WRITTEN BY CAROLINE TRIEU
ILLUSTRATED BY KANCHANOK INPRUNG

THAI CUISINE

RECIPES AND ANECDOTES FROM THAI GASTRONOMIC CULTURE

FIREFLY BOOKS

CONTENTS

THAI CUISINE

In Thailand, the first thing you ask when greeting someone is *kin khao ru yang* (กินข้าวหรือยัง), which means "have you eaten (rice) yet." It is a testament to Thai hospitality, which places the well-being of others and food, especially rice, at the center of life. If the answer to the question is "no," you will almost certainly be invited to eat. If the answer is "yes," you may still be invited to eat, especially if the people you are talking to are sitting around a table or enjoying a snack. In a country where food is everywhere, you need to be prepared to eat at any time!

AGRICULTURE IN THAILAND

Thailand is a vast territory with a varied terrain and climate. It is a major producer and exporter of agricultural products, and 40% of its land is devoted to farming. Agriculture is an important economic sector, employing more than a third of the working population.

AN AGRICULTURAL LAND

Northern Thailand is covered by forests and mid-sized mountains. The climate is cool and can even get cold, and a variety of ethnic groups live along its border with Burma and Laos. These peoples are traditionally farmers and grow a variety of grains, seeds and legumes, such as millet, sorghum, peanuts, beans, corn and rice as well as cassava and sugarcane.

ชาวนาคือ กระดูกสันหลังของชาติ
"Rice farmers are the backbone of the nation."

Popular Thai saying

The northeastern region borders the Mekong River along the arid Khorat Plateau, with its dry, impoverished soils. The northeast boasts a hot, dry climate for much of the year. It is the country's rice basket, and 60% of its land is devoted to the cultivation of rice. Sugarcane, cassava and rubber trees are also grown in large quantities.

Thailand's central plains boast fertile soil and a climate that favors agriculture, with ideal levels of sunshine and rainfall. This is the most densely populated area in Thailand, and it is considered the country's main agricultural region. Rice and sugarcane are the main crops grown here, along with palm trees and various other trees.

The south of the country is a peninsula with a tropical climate, with hot temperatures year-round and high humidity. Most of the land is used for groves of rubber and palm trees.

THE FOUR MAIN AGRICULTURAL SECTORS

Sugarcane has been grown in Thailand since the 14th century. Today, it is the country's largest agricultural product by volume. Thailand exports 80% of its sugar, making it the world's second-largest sugar exporter!

Sugar consumption in the region has exploded over the last 30 years, and people's eating habits are also changing. In our modern world, many people consume significant, even excessive, amounts of sugary drinks and dairy products. Refined sugar has also found its way into Thai kitchens, replacing the palm sugar they traditionally used. This has led to significant health problems, particularly among children, who are suffering increasingly from diabetes and obesity.

Rice is the most important agricultural product in Thailand, which is still one of the world's leading exporters of the grain. This sector alone employs 60% of the country's farmers and occupies half of its farmland. Rice is the staple food that feeds the population and is central to every meal. As such, it is revered throughout the country (see p. 20). Every grain of rice is respected, and rice is never wasted or scattered on the ground. Therefore, one always finishes the rice on one's plate. And if rice is fed to pets, it is placed in a bowl. Rice is also always given pride of place at banquets and ceremonies.

Cassava is originally from South America and was introduced to Thailand through the Ayutthaya Kingdom's trade with European settlers. It has now become an integral part of Thailand's culinary culture. It is widely used in the form of tapioca flour and tapioca pearls, particularly in desserts.

There are palm groves in Thailand dedicated to the production of palm sugar, which is traditionally used in Thai cuisine. These farms are predominantly located in the central region of Phetchaburi, which is renowned for the quality of its sugar. The south, meanwhile, is dominated by palm oil plantations: Thailand is the world's third-largest producer and exporter of palm oil, after Indonesia and Malaysia.

The palm oil industry has been growing steadily for the past 50 years, but it has had numerous environmental and human impacts. Demand for sustainable palm oil production is growing in Thailand, but it currently accounts for only 2% of production.

THE HISTORY OF THAI CUISINE

The Thai people began migrating down from what is now southern China in the 11th century. As they gradually moved south over the centuries, they encountered, and often waged war with, various peoples, primarily the Mon, the Khmer, the Burmese and the Malay. Lands and populations were absorbed and assimilated, enriching Thai culture and cuisine along the way.

THE MON LEGACY

The Mons were one of the first ethnic groups to populate Southeast Asia. We owe the expansion of Theravada Buddhism, the main religion of present-day Thailand, to them. They practiced riverine agriculture and irrigated rice cultivation, and they are thought to have migrated from southern China 2,000 to 3,000 years ago in search of fertile land. This is likely why they mainly settled along rivers. In Thailand, they mostly settled around the Chao Praya Basin, which is still the country's most fertile region.

THE KHMER LEGACY

Before the Ayutthaya Kingdom was established in Thailand in the 14th century, the Khmers, under the Angkor Empire, ruled the entire territory. Their society was highly sophisticated and enjoyed a refined cuisine. After the Khmers were defeated by the Ayutthaya, imperial Khmer cooks joined the palace kitchens, influencing local cuisine. The habits and customs of the Thai royal court and its table etiquette are said to have been passed down by Khmer nobility. There have always been many exchanges between the territories that are now Thailand and Cambodia, which share many ingredients and dishes, the origins of which are often the subject of much debate. The famous steamed curry custard wrapped in banana leaves (*hor mok*; ห่อหมก in Thai), for example, is said to have originated from the Cambodian *amok trei*.

THE FUSION CUISINE OF AYUTTHAYA

The Ayutthaya Kingdom, which dominated Thailand from the 14th to the 18th centuries, attracted numerous foreign delegations, from China and Japan to Europe via Persia. Trade with these countries had a considerable impact on Thai gastronomy.

THE PORTUGUESE INFLUENCE

The Portuguese were the first Europeans to come into contact with the Thai people, in the 16th century. Human and commercial exchanges flourished, and many products from the colonies of the Americas were introduced to Thailand, including tomatoes, potatoes, sweet potatoes, corn, papaya, peanuts and tobacco. Of these, the chili pepper is undoubtedly the most significant, completely reshaping Thailand's cuisine.

How significant is this European influence? In Bangkok, the Kudi Chin District has belonged to the Portuguese Catholic Church for 400 years! To thank the Portuguese for their allyship in the territorial wars against Burma, the emperor of Ayutthaya granted them land that is still occupied by their descendants today. Some of the classics of Portuguese cuisine can be found here, such as the famous custard tarts known as *pastéis de nata*.

Khanom farang (ขนมฝรั่ง), which means "foreign cake," evolved from Portuguese pastry-making techniques.

THE CHINESE INFLUENCE

Chinese and Thai history are inextricably linked. The first waves of Chinese immigrants arrived with the founding of the Ayutthaya Kingdom. King Rama I, who founded the Chakri dynasty over 200 years ago, himself had Chinese ancestry. The contributions of the Middle Kingdom to Thai culture and gastronomy are countless: soy sauce, tofu, noodles ... But wok cooking is perhaps the most iconic legacy and has become ubiquitous!

THE HARMONY OF FLAVORS

Thai cuisine is based on a harmony of five flavors: salty, sweet, sour, bitter and spicy. Each dish's profile combines two or three main flavors. What distinguishes a good dish from a great one is the marriage and balance of flavors!

Samrap (สำรับ): the full complement of dishes presented on the table.

A traditional meal always consists of a range of dishes served with rice. Each is designed to be eaten with rice in the same bite. These are called *khap khao*, which means "with rice." These dishes are highly seasoned but are balanced by the relatively neutral rice.

The overall selection of dishes should be harmonious, balanced and varied, featuring diverse textures, flavor profiles, temperatures, cooking styles and colors. Hot dishes include soup or liquid curries, creamy curries, stir-fried vegetables and meat or fish. There are also room-temperature dishes, such as appetizers, salads and a dish of *nam prik* accompanied by a platter of herbs and raw vegetables. You simply need to ensure that all flavors are represented and that there are dishes with and without chili to suit every taste.

This quest for harmony goes far beyond the plate and is best understood in light of the relationships that individuals maintain in society. Thais like to joke, keep a light tone and have a sense of humor in everyday conversations. The language even has a gesture of politeness to soften the end of each sentence: *ka* (ค่ะ) for women and *krap* (ครับ) for men. Getting angry or raising your voice is frowned upon. In the event a conflict arises, we don't get angry at the other person, as this would be tantamount to publicly humiliating them. You have to keep smiling and stay calm, "keep your heart cold," as we say in Thai (*jai yen*; ใจเย็น). This attitude can often be enough to lighten the mood. Harmony must reign, whatever the circumstances. That's why Thailand is known as the Land of Smiles.

This quest for harmony also entails concern for others in all circumstances, known as *kreng jai* (เกรงใจ). At the table, this is expressed through various etiquette rules. For example, you only fill your plate with a small amount of one or two dishes, ensuring there is enough left for other guests (see also p. 39).

ROYAL CUISINE

The royal family, one of the pillars of the nation, have shaped Thailand's gastronomy over centuries. Dishes conceived in royal kitchens have made today's Thai cuisine famous and appreciated the world over. And while these elaborate, elegant, complex and time-consuming dishes were once the privilege of high society, they are now on the plates of the entire population.

THE ETIQUETTE OF ROYAL CUISINE

Celebrity chef McDang is of royal blood and grew up eating at the queen's table. He explains that royal cuisine is much the same as that of central Thailand but follows precise rules and maintains very high standards. First, only the finest, freshest ingredients are used. They must be perfectly deboned and cut into bite-sized pieces. Flavors are perfectly balanced so that none dominates the others, and "extreme" tastes are strictly avoided. So-called "jungle food" (*ahan pa*; อาหารป่า) and overpowering smells, such as certain fermented fish sauces (*pla ra*; ปลาร้า) are also avoided. Last but not least, the dishes are beautifully presented, and fruits and vegetables are meticulously carved.

มัสมั่นแกงแก้วตา หอมยี่หร่ารสร้อนแรง
ชายใดได้กลืนแกง แรงอยากให้ใฝ่ฝันหา

"Your massaman curry is cumin-scented and has a fiery flavor. Any man who has ever tasted this soup would desire you."

Excerpt from the poem
"Kaphae chom khrueng khao wan"
by Rama II

A LITERARY CUISINE

When Rama II was still a young prince, he wrote a poem to express his love for Princess Bunrot, who would later become his wife. It is an ode to 17 sweet dishes and 14 savory dishes made by his beloved, praising how delightful they are. This poem, entitled "Kaphae chom khrueng khao wan" (กาพย์เห่ชมเครื่องคาวหวาน) is a literary masterpiece and is still taught in Thai schools.

Princess Bunrot, who became Queen Consort Sri Suriyendra, played a major role in the evolution of Thai cuisine, incorporating skills from other countries. She also adapted foreign recipes to suit the Thai palate, such as *massaman* curry, which has become a classic dish.

NON-VEGETARIAN BUDDHISM

The subject of vegetarianism in Buddhism is at the heart of an endless debate that divides the community. During his lifetime, Buddha was apparently not a vegetarian and would not have asked his disciples to follow such a diet. His last meal even consisted of an offering of pork. The sacred texts (Vinaya) recounting the Buddha's life and teachings indicate that he made a distinction between the three "pure" meats and the ten other "impure" meats.

DIFFERENCES ACROSS THE BRANCHES OF BUDDHISM

The practice of vegetarianism in Buddhism is said to have emerged only centuries after the religion began to be practiced, with the evolution of the precept of non-violence known as Ahiṃsa. This was followed by the current Mahayana branch of Buddhism, which spread first to China and then to Vietnam, Korea and Japan. The Buddhism practiced in Thailand belongs to the Theravada branch, which is the oldest in Southeast Asia. It is believed to be closer to the Buddha's original doctrine and does not impose strict abstinence from meat.

In Thailand, monks eat only once per day, during the morning almsgiving known as *tak bat* (ตักบาตร). They walk barefoot through the streets bordering the temple where they live, accepting food offered by the faithful. The practice of *tak bat* also provides an insight into the non-vegetarian Buddhism observed by Theravada monks. Following in the Buddha's footsteps, monks live a life of material detachment: When begging, they must accept donations of food without choosing what to eat.

The practice of almsgiving (tak bat; ตักบาตร)

"Fish and meat are pure if the following three conditions are met: It has not been seen, heard or suspected" (meaning the animal must not have been killed specifically for the monk).

Excerpt from Vinaya

THE HEALTH AND DIET OF MONKS

The Buddhist religion, which is followed by almost 95% of Thailand's population, and the royal family are the great pillars on which Thai society was founded. Practicing almsgiving is considered a good deed that allows the faithful to accumulate karmic merit (*tham boun*; ทำบุญ) for their next reincarnation or for a deceased loved one. The faithful often prepare the deceased's favorite foods, which are often very sweet. A study conducted by Chulalongkorn University in 2016 revealed that half of all monks are overweight and suffer from high cholesterol and diabetes! In response, the government, which covers the monks' medical expenses, has launched the "Making Merit or Creating Hurt" campaign, which is designed to encourage the faithful to choose more nutritionally responsible foods for their offerings.

VEGETARIAN CUISINE

Thailand is not known for its vegetarian cuisine. Quite the opposite. With fish sauce and shrimp paste at the heart of many seasonings, it can be hard to find a dish without traces of animal protein. There is, however, an ancient tradition that was introduced by the Chinese Buddhist community over 200 years ago: *Ahan je* (อาหารเจ) is even more restrictive than either vegetarian or vegan cuisine. An annual festival dedicated to *ahan je* is celebrated throughout the country. To mark the occasion, street vendors change their usual menu to entirely *je* offerings!

WHAT IS EATING *JE*?

In Thailand, we say that we are eating *je* or *kin je* (กินเจ) to indicate that we are not eating meat. This tradition is derived from the restrictive diet followed by Chinese Buddhist monks, which differs from that of Thai monks. The civilian population does not follow the same diet in daily life, but they do observe it during the Thesakan Kin Je (เทศกาลกินเจ) festival, which begins on the ninth day of the ninth month of the lunar calendar and lasts for nine days. There are many Thais of Chinese descent, making this festival a national event.

Like a vegan diet, the *je* diet prohibits the consumption of animal protein and meat, so it excludes dairy products and honey. It goes even further, though, excluding foods with a strong taste or smell, such as garlic, onions, shallots, scallions, leeks and tobacco leaves. These foods are said to disrupt the body's energies and inflame emotions.

Other than during the festival, vegetarian cuisine is not featured prominently in the Thai culinary scene. It is usually served in modern restaurants in big cities or at some traditional food stalls, called *ran khao kaeng* (ร้านข้าวแกง), where rice plates are served with a variety of dishes from which diners can choose. Some stalls are entirely dedicated to *je* cuisine, but most only serve a few vegetarian dishes. The best way to ensure your dish is vegetarian is to ask.

SOME VEGETARIAN SPECIALTIES

Je dishes are quite varied, reproducing visually the soups, curries, stir-fries, stews, salads and *nam prik* platters of the traditional Thai culinary repertoire. Mushrooms and tofu are often used in place of meat, and soy sauce is used as a seasoning.

Vegetarian sausages
Sai krok je
ไส้กรอกเจ

Vegetable spring rolls
Po pia je
เปาะเปี๊ยะเจ

Chinese broccoli stir-fry
Pad pak kaneng
ผัดผักแขนง

Seasoned mushrooms
Hed prung rod
เห็ดปรุงรส

Sweet-and-sour tofu stir-fry
Pad priew wan taohu
ผัดเปรี้ยวหวานเต้าหู้

Mushroom *nam prik*
Nam prik hed
น้ำพริกเห็ด

EVERYDAY CUISINE

Traditional Thai meals bring the entire family together around the table. Once called *samrab ahaan* (สำรับอาหาร) but now more commonly called *khap khao* (กับข้าว), these meals feature a variety of dishes and rice is always included. In fact, *khap khao* means "with rice." While eating out has become increasingly common in Thailand, families still tend to gather for dinner. In the fast-paced lives of city dwellers, it is common for takeout food from street stalls or delivered from restaurants to make up part or all of the meal. In more rural areas, people tend to prepare their meals at home. Whatever the lifestyle, there is always an abundance of food on the table!

RICE

Rice is at the center of life in Thailand, with an average resident consuming around 350 pounds (150 kg) per year. Rice is not considered a side dish. It is placed at the center of the table and forms the basis of most meals. Rice allows other dishes and flavors to express themselves. Its importance is such that "to eat" translates to *kin khao* (กินข้าว), literally "to eat rice," and it is celebrated at all major life events. This grain is also central to the country's economy: average production is 20 to 25 million tons per year. Half of this is exported, making Thailand one of the world's leading exporters of rice.

THE SIX MAIN TYPES OF RICE

Jasmine rice (*khao hom mali*; ข้าวหอมมะลิ) is the most popular and well-known Thai rice. Its name comes from the jasmine-like whiteness of the grain. Its delicate fragrance is reminiscent of pandan leaves.

White sticky rice (*khao niew kao*; ข้าวเหนียวขาว) is the second most popular and consumed rice in Thailand. Also called glutinous rice, it is widely used in desserts and in the cuisines of the north and northeast of the country.

Black sticky rice (*khao niew dam*; ข้าวเหนียวดำ) is similar to white sticky rice but has a denser texture. It is also cooked by steaming, usually with white sticky rice, at a ratio of three parts black rice to one part white rice. The rices are soaked and cooked together.

Brown rice (*khao klong*; ข้าวกล้อง) is a whole-grain rice from the jasmine or common long-grain rice family. It contains more nutrients than white jasmine rice but is much less popular.

Riceberry (*khao rice berry*; ข้าวไรซ์เบอร์รี่) is a recently created hybrid variety of whole-grain rice. It has a deep purple color and is becoming increasingly popular, as it is considered a superfood.

There are many varieties of **white rice** (*khao kao*; ข้าวขาว) in Thailand. These are neither jasmine rice nor sticky rice, but common white long-grain rice. These rices are much cheaper and are eaten daily by the general population.

JASMINE RICE

KHAO HOM MALI

ข้าวหอมมะลิ

Yield: 4 servings
Prep time: 30 minutes

- 1½ cups (375 ml) uncooked jasmine rice

1 Rinse the rice three times with plenty of water to remove excess starch. Drain thoroughly.

2 Put the rinsed and drained rice in a saucepan or rice cooker and add an equal volume of water.

3 Cover and start cooking. If using a saucepan, cook for 20 minutes on medium heat without opening the lid.

4 Turn off the heat and let the cooked rice sit for 10 more minutes, covered, to allow it to absorb all the moisture.

STICKY RICE

KHAO NIEW

ข้าวเหนียว

Yield: 4 servings
Prep time: 30 minutes
Soak time: 4 hours (or overnight)

- 1½ cups (375 ml) sticky rice

1 Soak the rice in plenty of water for at least 4 hours.

2 Drain the rice and place it in a bamboo basket suitable for cooking sticky rice.

3 Bring a large pot of water to a boil, and then place the basket on top, sealed with a lid. If the lid does not seal tightly, wrap the pot in a dish towel to prevent steam from escaping.

4 Cook for 25 minutes. Halfway through the cooking time, toss the rice by shaking the basket using a sharp motion to ensure the grains cook evenly.

5 Once the rice is cooked, spread it out on a tray to let any excess steam evaporate, and then place it in the bamboo basket to keep it warm.

Mae Phosop (แม่โพสพ)
This ancient deity, also known as Mae Kwan Khao (mother of the prosperity of rice) and Mae Khao (mother of rice), originates from Thailand's pre-Buddhist animist beliefs. Ceremonies and offerings are dedicated to her throughout the country to ensure her blessings and a good rice harvest. Rice paddies are considered Mae Phosop's womb giving birth to harvests. It is customary to never waste a single grain of rice during a meal, as a sign of respect for the nourishment offered by Mae Phosop.

NOODLES

Rice noodles and egg noodles are very popular with Thais, who enjoy them in soups, stir-fries and even deep-fried. The history of rice vermicelli (*khanom jin*; ขนมจีน) dates back to the Mon people, and they have been eaten in Thailand since time immemorial. The other noodles, however, were imported by successive waves of Chinese immigrants. Once eaten only by the Chinese, these noodles, such those used for *pad thai*, are now a source of national pride and help promote Thai gastronomy around the world.

STIR-FRIED NOODLES

Stir-fried rice noodles with soy sauce
Pad see ew
ผัดซีอิ๊ว

Stir-fried rice vermicelli with soy sauce
Pad woon sen
ผัดวุ้นเส้น

DEEP-FRIED NOODLES

Sweet-and-sour crispy noodles
Mi krob
หมี่กรอบ

Noodle salad
Yam mama
ยำมาม่า

NOODLE SOUPS

Egg noodle soup with barbecue pork and wontons
Ba mi moo dang
บะหมี่หมูแดง

Soup with rice noodle rolls, clear broth and pork offal
Kuay jap nam sai
กวยจั๊บน้ำใส

THE DIFFERENT NOODLES

RICE NOODLES

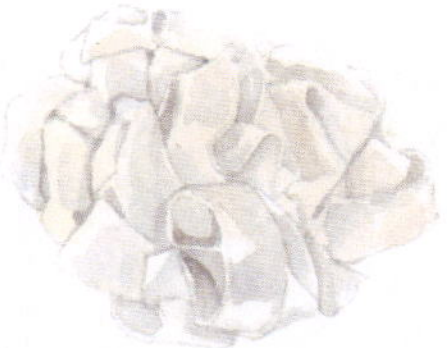

Broad noodles (*kouay tiew sen yai*; เส้นใหญ่) are found in dishes like *pad see ew*, which is stir-fried noodles with soy sauce.

Thin noodles (*kouay tiew sen mi*; เส้นหมี่) are used in deep-fried noodle dishes such as *mi krob*.

Medium noodles (*kouay tiew sen lek*; เส้นเล็ก) are also known as *sen pad thai* and are a main feature of the iconic national dish *pad thai*.

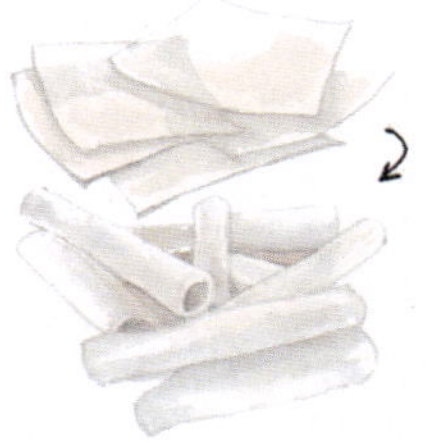

Rice noodle rolls (*kouay jap*; กวยจั๊บ) are used in the noodle soup of the same name.

WHEAT NOODLES

Wheat noodles (*sen ba mi*; เส้นบะหมี่) are often served in a soup with barbecue pork called *moo dang*.

Mung bean vermicelli (*woon sen*; วุ้นเส้น) are translucent noodles that are equally delicious in soups, stir-fries and salads.

Instant ramen noodles (*mama*; มาม่า) are served in both *pad mama* stir-fry and *yam mama* noodle salad.

Fermented rice vermicelli (*khanom jin*; ขนมจีน) accompany all kinds of curries. Their long strands symbolize longevity, giving them a place of honor at weddings and other celebrations. They are often colored blue, pink, yellow and green for special occasions.

HERBS AND AROMATICS

Thailand encompasses a vast territory with different climates and landscapes. The numerous herbs consumed throughout the country vary greatly and contribute to the richness of its cuisine. They are used both raw and cooked to flavor soups, curries, stir-fries and salads. Garlic and scallions (or green onions) are the basic aromatics used in nearly every recipe. Seasonings often include the fruity acidity of lime or other citrus, tamarind or pineapple. Here is a selection of the herbs and other aromatics most often encountered in Thai cuisine.

THE TRINITY OF THAI CUISINE

The combination of Kaffir lime leaves, galangal and lemongrass form Thailand's culinary identity. These essential flavors appear in many dishes, such as the famous *tom yam* soup.

Kaffir lime
Bai makrut
ใบมะกรูด
This tangy citrus fruit is a cousin of the lime. Thai cooks infuse its leaves whole in soups and finely chop them to garnish and flavor dishes. The zest is used in curry pastes. Its flesh is not very juicy and highly acidic, so it is rarely used.

Galangal
Kha
ข่า
It is a rhizome, like ginger, but has a completely different flavor and aroma — fresh and powerful. It flavors soups, curries and many other dishes.

Lemongrass
Takrai
ตะไคร้
Lemongrass stems are infused into soups, broths and curries. Its aroma is refreshingly lemony.

Holy basil
Bai kaprao
ใบกะเพรา

It has a peppery taste and is particularly good in stir-fries, such as the spicy national dish *pad kaprao*!

Sweet Thai basil
Bai horapha
ใบโหระพา

It is widely used and much appreciated for its aniseed flavor, which goes well in both red and green curries.

Lemon basil
Bai menglak
ใบแมงลัก

As its name suggests, this basil has a lemony aroma that is ideal for certain curries, such as yellow curry or fish curry with turmeric.

Garlic scapes
Dok guichai
ดอกกุยช่าย

With their fragrance of chives and garlic, garlic scapes are mainly used in stir-fries. The stems can be used to flavor dishes such as *pad thai.*

Cilantro
Pak chi
ผักชี

This is one of the essential elements of Thai cuisine. Nothing is wasted: The roots flavor broths, marinades and curries, while the stalks and leaves garnish and flavor a variety of dishes.

Culantro
Pak chi farang
ผักชีฝรั่ง

It has a strong herbaceous flavor and is used to garnish soups, noodle dishes and the *laap* meat salads popular in northern Thailand.

Pandan leaves
Bai toei
ใบเตย

It flavors broths and grilled meats and is used as both a flavoring and coloring in rice and coconut milk desserts. It can also be artfully braided and displayed in living spaces so it can diffuse its fragrance.

Scallion or green onion
Ton hom
ต้นหอม

It is a ubiquitous ingredient that garnishes and flavors a wide variety of dishes.

Leaf or Chinese celery
Kun chai
ขึ้นฉ่าย

This celery has much thinner stems than the one we normally find in the West. It can be stir-fried in a wok, steamed with fish or used in salads. It provides a delightful aroma to many dishes.

VEGETABLES

Thais eat a huge variety of vegetables. The eggplant and cabbage families are particularly well represented. Some unripe fruits are also cooked as vegetables. Here is a small selection of the most popular vegetables in Thai cuisine.

Thai and Indian eggplant
Makhua phrao
มะเขือเปราะ
These small, round eggplants can be green, purple, white or yellow. They are eaten raw for their crunchiness. When cooked, their flesh melts in the mouth.

Pea eggplant (also called turkey berry)
Makhua puang
มะเขือพวง
These tiny eggplants are often served raw on a platter with fresh herbs and vegetables to accompany *nam prik* or curry dishes. They stay crunchy even when cooked.

Thai long green eggplant
Makhua yao
มะเขือยาว
These eggplants measure 10 to 12 inches (25 to 30 cm) and can be stir-fried in a wok or grilled on a barbecue for salads and *nam prik*.

Chinese broccoli
Pak kana
ผักคะน้า
It is often stir-fried with crispy pork (*pak kana moo krob*) or with noodles, such as in *pad see ew*.

Water spinach
Pak bong
ผักบุ้ง
Often served stir-fried with garlic and chilies, water spinach is also cooked in soups and curries.

White cabbage
Kalampli
กะหล่ำปลี
Presented either raw as part of a vegetable platter or stir-fried, *kalampli* is very popular in Thai cuisine.

Long beans
Tuo fak yao
ถั่วฝักยาว
This very crunchy, neutral-tasting bean can be eaten raw, in *yam* salads or stir-fried.

Bitter beans
Sator
สะตอ
Also known as "stink bean," this vegetable has a lingering bitter flavor. It is widely used in dishes associated with southern Thailand.

Bitter melon
Mara
มะระ
As its name suggests, this is an extremely bitter vegetable! It is not suitable for sensitive palates. It can be eaten raw on its own or in salads or cooked in stir-fries or soups.

Acacia leaves
Cha om
ชะอม
These leaves have a very pronounced bitterness and are most often used in *khai jiew cha om* omelets. They are also eaten raw with *nam prik* or in salads, curries or soups.

Bamboo shoots
No mai
หน่อไม้
Bamboo shoots are very popular. They are blanched and then served in *yam* salads, soups, curries or stir-fries. They retain a crunchy texture, even after being cooked.

Green papaya
Malako dib
มะละกอดิบ
Picked before the fruit ripens, green papaya is prepared like a vegetable. It has a neutral flavor and crunchy flesh. Particularly appreciated in the famous *som tam* salad, it is also used in the iconic southern curry *kaeng som*.

SPICES

Spices only gradually became part of Thailand's culinary landscape. Many spices first appeared with Silk Road traders crossing the north of the country, and they then spread to more southernly communities through Indo-Malaysian influences and Chinese immigrants. Today, spices play a vital role in the country's gastronomy. Some recipes, such as *massaman* curry, call for a wide range of spices, but the most common are white pepper, coriander seeds and cumin seeds.

RHIZOMES

Ginger
King
ขิง
Ginger appears predominantly in dishes with Chinese origins, such as stir-fries. Young ginger (*king on*; ขิงอ่อน) is bitter but not sharp and is usually served fresh or pickled.

Turmeric
Kamin
ขมิ้น
With its earthy, tart flavor, turmeric is used in many curries in both the north and south of the country. It gives dishes a characteristic yellow color.

Fingerroot
Krachai
กระชาย
It has a distinctively fresh, medicinal flavor that goes well with fish, as it can neutralize fishy odors.

DRIED SPICES

Cumin seeds
Maled yira
เมล็ดยี่หร่า
Characteristic of southern cuisine, cumin seeds flavor curry pastes.

Coriander seeds
Luk pak chi
เม็ดผักชี
They are used to make curry pastes and flavor marinades and stocks.

White peppercorns
Prik thai
พริกไทย
White peppercorns and fresh green peppercorns are the only peppers regularly used in Thai cuisine.

CHILIES

Chilies are certainly emblematic of Thai cuisine, but did you know they are not native to the region? Portuguese missionaries brought them from the Americas in the 16th century. Before that, Thais used peppercorns to spice up their cuisine. Thai chili varieties have since been developed and are the pride of the country.

Bird's eye chilies
Prik ki nuu suan
พริกขี้หนู
This small, very hot pepper is known in Thai as "mouse poop chili." Thais are very fond of hot peppers and do not hesitate to bite into them.

Jinda chilies
Prik jinda
พริกจินดา
These popular chilies can be red or green. They are longer and more fragrant than bird's eye chilies and not as hot.

Spur chilies
Prik chi fa
พริกชี้ฟ้า
These long green or red chilies are not very hot. They are used to color dishes and curry pastes.

Dried chilies
Prik heng
พริกแดง
A variety of chilies are dried, and they have many uses. The longer ones, such as *prik chi fa*, add color to curries, while the shorter ones, such as *prik jinda*, add flavor and spiciness.

Chili flakes
Prik bon
พริกป่น
Flakes of dried and roasted bird's eye chilies spice up a wide range of recipes. They are the Thai equivalent of black pepper and grace every table.

Green peppercorns
Prik thai on
พริกไทยอ่อน
Fresh green peppercorns are not part of the chili family, but they do have a spicy flavor and were used long before chilies were introduced to the region.

THE ART OF SEASONING

Thai cuisine incorporates a number of sauces and condiments, both in the preparation of dishes and to customize the flavor once at the table. Seasoning is a veritable art in the quest for balanced flavors. It is what undoubtedly distinguishes a good dish from an excellent one! The first written recipes rarely mentioned quantities, as if to leave the cook free to achieve this perfect balance on their own.

THAILAND'S ICONS

Fish sauce (*nam pla;* น้ำปลา)
Found in nearly every dish, fish sauce is a superstar of Thai cuisine. In fact, it is the only sauce that originates from Thailand. It is made from salted anchovies that are fermented for three to twelve months, from which the juice is extracted. It is used as a kind of "table salt" and is also an ingredient in dipping sauces for meats and fish.

Shrimp paste (*kapi;* กะปิ)
Kapi is one of the oldest Thai foodstuffs. It was originally used to preserve shrimp through fermentation. Today, it is used in a wide range of recipes, including curry pastes. It is an essential element of Thai gastronomy.

CHINESE SAUCES

These sauces were popularized by the immigrant Chinese community, which is no doubt why they are particularly popular in stir-fries and Chinese-Thai dishes.

Light soy sauce (*si ew khao;* ซีอิ๊วขาว)
This salty sauce made from soybeans is a must for stir-fries. It is used both while preparing dishes and to season them at the table. Light soy sauce can be used as a vegetarian substitute for fish sauce.

Dark soy sauce (*si ew dam;* ซีอิ๊วดำ)
Thick in consistency, dark soy sauce tastes similar to molasses. It gives a beautiful color to dishes. It is used in marinades for meats and in sauces for dipping.

Seasoning sauce (*prung rod;* ซอสปรุงรส)
The Golden Mountain brand of soy sauce has become its own entity but is similar to light soy sauce.

OTHER SAUCES

Oyster sauce (*hoi nang rom*; ซอสหอยนางรม)
Oyster sauce is an indispensable ingredient in stir-fries. Its thick texture and salty, slightly sweet and umami-rich flavor enhances any vegetable or meat stir-fry.

Fermented soybean paste
(*tao jiew*; เต้าเจี้ยว)
This Thai version of miso is not used as frequently as these other sauces, but it is integral to a number of dishes, such as the sauce that accompanies *khao man kai* and certain stir-fries.

WHERE DOES SRIRACHA SAUCE COME FROM?

Sriracha sauce (ซอสศรีราชา), also known as "Asia's spicy ketchup," takes its name from the stretch of coast where it is said it was first sold in Thailand, in 1949.

But it was Thanom Chakkapak's introduction of *Sriracha Panich*, based on her father's recipe, that made the sauce a household name. Sriracha became a resounding success across the continent, particularly in Vietnam. In 1975 David Tran, a Vietnamese immigrant who had fled the war, launched the sauce in the United States. Huy Fong sriracha sauce, recognized by its rooster mascot, was an immediate success.

In Thailand, sriracha sauce accompanies fried foods such as fried chicken, fried wontons, vegetable fritters and *khai jiew* (ไข่เจียว) omelet.

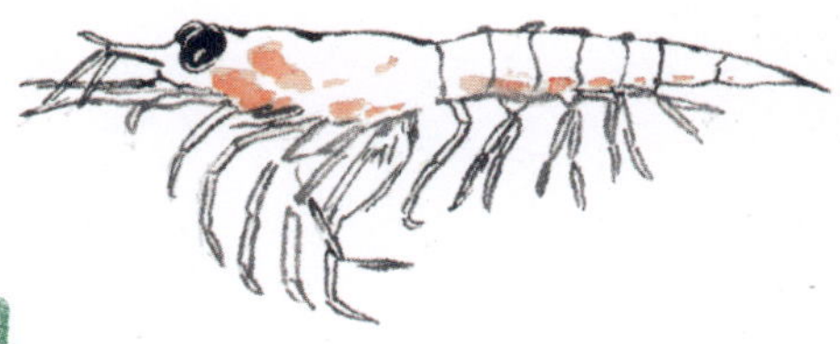

CONDIMENTS AT THE TABLE

The condiments commonly found at the table are called *krueng pwong* (เครื่องพวง). They are often presented in a set that represents the four essential flavors: fish sauce with or without chili (salty), confectioners' sugar (sweet), chili vinegar (sour) and chili flakes (spicy). These condiments are primarily used to season noodle soups to each individual's taste, but they also season many other dishes. They are the salt and pepper of Thailand! Other condiments are also often served with meats and fish and as dips for finger foods and fried foods. These are the quintessential Thai condiments.

Fish sauce
Nam pla
น้ำปลา
It is also served with *prik nam pla* peppers.

Confectioners' sugar
Nam tan sai
น้ำตาลทราย

Chili flakes
Prik bon
พริกป่น

Chili vinegar
Prik nam som
พริกน้ำส้ม

NAM JIM KAI (น้ำจิ้มไก่)

This sweet-and-sour sauce goes well with fried foods, such as fried chicken. Sweet and not overly spicy, it is a favorite among children!

Yield: ¾ cup (175 ml)
Prep time: 10 minutes

- 1 spur chili or other Thai chili
- 3 cloves garlic
- ⅓ cup (75 ml) rice vinegar or white vinegar
- 1 cup (250 ml) confectioners' sugar
- ½ tsp. (2 ml) salt
- 1 tbsp. (15 ml) cornstarch, diluted with 1 tbsp. (15 ml) water

1. Blend the chili and garlic with ⅓ cup (75 ml) water. Transfer the mixture to a saucepan.
2. In a bowl, stir together the vinegar, sugar, salt and diluted cornstarch to combine, and then add to the mixture in the saucepan.
3. Heat the mixture over high heat until it thickens.

AJAD (อาจาด)

Also called *achard,* it is a combination of vegetables prepared in brine. These pickles are often served with skewers of meat, fish fritters and dishes popular with Thailand's Muslim community. This cool condiment is not spicy and refreshes the palate when eating fatty dishes and sauces.

Yield: 1 bowl
Prep time: 5 minutes

- 1-inch (3 cm) piece of cucumber
- 1 or 2 chilies (optional)
- 1 shallot
- 2 tbsp. (30 ml) white vinegar
- 1 tbsp. (15 ml) granulated sugar
- 1 pinch salt

1. Peel the cucumber and dice it finely. Mince the chili and shallot.
2. Dissolve the sugar in 2 tbsp. (30 ml) water in a saucepan over low heat.
3. Allow the sugar mixture to cool, and then add the remaining ingredients.

NAM JIM SEAFOOD (น้ำจิ้มซีฟู้ด)

As its name suggests, this lemony sauce is excellent with fish and seafood.

Yield: 1 bowl
Prep time: 5 minutes

- 6 bird's eye chilies, minced
- 2 cloves garlic, minced
- 2 tbsp. (30 ml) minced cilantro stems
- 3 tbsp. (45 ml) fish sauce
- 3 tbsp. (45 ml) lime juice
- ½ tsp. (2 ml) granulated sugar

1. In a small bowl, stir the ingredients to combine.

NAM JIM JEOW (น้ำจิ้มแจ่ว)

This is a popular condiment to accompany grilled meats and sticky rice.

Yield: 1 bowl
Prep time: 10 minutes
Cook time: 2 minutes

- 2 tbsp. (30 ml) uncooked sticky rice
- 1 shallot
- 2 tbsp. (30 ml) palm sugar
- ¼ cup (60 ml) fish sauce
- 2 tbsp. (30 ml) tamarind pulp
- 2 tbsp. (30 ml) lime juice
- 2 tsp. (10 ml) ground chili peppers
- 2 tbsp. (30 ml) minced scallion, green parts only (optional)
- 2 tbsp. (30 ml) minced fresh cilantro

1. In a dry frying pan, toast the sticky rice so it is evenly browned.
2. Blend the toasted rice to a powder (*khao khua*).
3. Finely mince the shallot.
4. Chop the palm sugar so it can be incorporated into the sauce.
5. To prepare the sauce, combine the liquid ingredients and then add the sugar. Stir until the sugar dissolves. Add the ground chilies, rice powder and minced shallot.
6. Sprinkle the minced scallion and cilantro on top just before serving.

PRIK NAM PLA (พริกน้ำปลา)

Yield: 1 bowl
Prep time: 5 minutes

- 8 red or green bird's eye chilies (or as many as you like)
- 4 cloves garlic
- ¾ cup (175 ml) fish sauce

1. Thinly slice the chilies and mince the garlic.
2. Combine them with the fish sauce.

Ajad

Nam jim seafood

Nam jim jeow

Prik nam pla

FERMENTED FISH SAUCES

Fermentation is an ancient process for enhancing and preserving foodstuffs that is still widely used in Thailand. Shrimp, freshwater fish and saltwater fish are available in abundance and are the favorite products to ferment. But vegetables and meats can also be fermented. Fermented fish sauces and shrimp pastes are strongly flavored condiments that are essential components of the country's gastronomy. They provided saltiness and umami to dishes long before the more recent introduction of soy sauce. Each region has developed its own variations based on the available fish, production methods and local customs.

FISH SAUCE (*NAM PLA*; น้ำปลา)

Anchovies are often the fish used to make *nam pla*. Being small, they are less suitable for consumption any other way. The fish is salted and fermented in covered containers for six months to two years. As the fish breaks down through the action of the enzymes it contains, it releases its celebrated juices. Once the desired level of fermentation has been achieved, the liquid is extracted, filtered and bottled. It is sometimes boiled to ensure pasteurization and sweetened with sugar. When a recipe calls simply for "fish sauce," it is almost certainly calling for *nam pla*.

There are several grades of fish sauce. The dregs of the first fermentation can be diluted with salt water and then filtered again. This operation may be repeated several times, which leads to a loss of flavor in favor of salt.

PLA RA FISH SAUCE (ปลาร้า) AND *NAM BUDU* FISH SAUCE (น้ำบูดู)

Other examples of fermented fish sauces are *pla ra*, consumed in northeastern Thailand and Laos, and *nam budu*, consumed in southern Thailand and Malaysia. Unlike *nam pla*, these sauces are not filtered and therefore contain the flesh of the fish, making them much thicker and stronger in flavor.

Any river fish can be used to prepare *pla ra*. The fish is cleaned, gutted and sliced before being salted, covered with water and left to ferment. After this first step, which can be more or less long, rice bran, rice powder or toasted sticky rice is added. The fish is then left to ferment again. Fermentation times can vary widely, from a few months to a year or more. This is a popular condiment in the cuisine of the Isan region, where it is used to make green papaya salad (*som tam pla ra*).

Nam budu is made from anchovies and is sometimes seasoned with palm sugar and tamarind paste. The fish is then salted, placed in a terra-cotta jar and covered with water. A lid is put on the jar, and the preparation is left to ferment for six or seven months in the sun. This sauce is typical of southern Thai cuisine and is an important ingredient in *khao yam* rice salad, the region's signature breakfast.

SHRIMP PASTE (*KAPI*; กะปิ)

Fermented shrimp paste is one of the oldest foods consumed by Thai people. It is still a staple in Thai cuisine today and is the basis of all *nam prik*, the popular condiment dips served with rice and a variety of vegetables. *Kapi* is also used in most curry pastes.

The buttery, dark purple paste is made from a mixture of salt and krill, a small crustacean similar to shrimp. The krills (*koy*; เคย) are salted and then left to ferment for one or two days. They are then dried and ground into a paste, which is placed in covered jars and left to ferment for up to six months. *Kapi* has a very strong flavor and smell. Only a small amount is needed to season dishes and give them depth.

COOKING TOOLS

Traditional Thai cuisine is based on the preparation of a ground paste (*kreung tam*; เครื่องตำ) composed of chilies, herbs and spices. This paste is the base of every dish! Everything from *nam prik* dips to salads, soups and curries require grinding foods. The only real exception is infused soups. As such, the mortar and pestle (*krok le sak*; ครกและสาก) is without a doubt the oldest and most essential tool in Thai gastronomy.

There are two main types of mortars and pestles

- Wooden or clay mortars with a wooden pestle: these lightweight materials keep delicate foods from turning to mush, preserving more texture. They are used to prepare salads, sauces and *nam prik*.
- Granite mortars and pestles: these heavier materials are ideal to grind even the hardest foods to a smooth puree for curry pastes.

The clay charcoal barbecue (*tao than*; เตาถ่าน) is also an ancient tool that is still widely used. It can be used to grill foods, boil soups in a pot or stir-fry ingredients in a wok. The *tao than* is popular in more rural areas but is also found on the streets of Bangkok, where some street vendors still practice this style of cooking.

Bamboo baskets (*kradip khao niew*; กระติ๊บข้าวเหนียว) keep cooked sticky rice warm and prevent it from drying out. At mealtimes, the basket of rice is simply placed on the table.

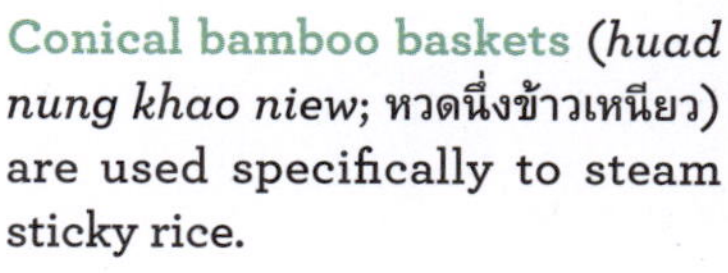

Conical bamboo baskets (*huad nung khao niew*; หวดนึ่งข้าวเหนียว) are used specifically to steam sticky rice.

Clay pots (*maw din*; หม้อดิน) were traditionally used to cook everything from rice to soups to curries. Today, rice is usually cooked in an electric pressure cooker, while soups and curries are prepared in saucepans. However, the clay pot remains the traditional vessel for *tchim tchoum* (จิ้มจุ่ม), which is a fondue composed of meats and vegetables cooked in a broth.

Brass pans (*krata tong luang*; กระทะทองเหลือง) are an indispensable classic for making desserts. Their exceptional ability to conduct heat is ideal for the long cook times of syrupy desserts. Some also use a *krata tong luang* to make curries.

The ubiquitous wok is called a *krata* or *krata chin* (กระทะจีน), which translates to "Chinese frying pan." The name refers to the pan's origins, as it was brought to Thailand by Chinese immigrants. It has since conquered the entire country. It is used to cook a wide variety of stir-fried dishes: rice, noodles, vegetables and meat. But what do we mean by "stir-frying in a wok"? It is simply a matter of keeping the ingredients moving so their surfaces remain in contact with the heat and cook evenly and quickly without sticking to the pan. Woks can also be used to deep-fry foods.

The *moo krata* (หมูกระทะ) combines Korean barbecue and Chinese hot pot: pieces of pork fat are used to oil the stone grill in the center, where meats are cooked. The perimeter is curved inward and filled with broth, in which noodles, vegetables and seafood are cooked. This tool is so popular in Thailand that there are specialty restaurants where it is the only thing served! These restaurants are popular destinations for nights out, since they encourage conversation and socialization.

CUTLERY

HOW SHOULD I EAT WITH MY FINGERS?

Traditionally, Thai meals were eaten with the fingers, and diners sat on the floor. All dishes were served at room temperature to avoid burns, and food was chopped to make it easy to grab.

1 Diners rinse their fingers in a bowl of water at the table.

2 Diners grab a mouthful of rice and shape it using three fingers (the thumb, forefinger and middle finger).

3 They then layer other foods onto the rice before gently bringing it to their mouth.

Today, this is still the most widespread way to eat in rural areas, and it is how northerners eat dishes with sticky rice and how southerners enjoy a curry accompanied by pan-fried bread.

THE FORK AND SPOON

European cutlery first appeared on royal tables in the 19th century, as a result of foreign trade. Utensils were adopted by the nobility, who found it more sophisticated to eat "European style." In the 1930s, Prime Minister Plaek Phibunsongkhram launched a series of measures to modernize Thailand, including the adoption of cutlery. Since then, the spoon and fork have become the norm at Thai tables. A knife is not necessary, however, as all food is served precut.

CHOPSTICKS ARE SINGLE USE ONLY!

Chopsticks are used exclusively to eat noodles, a custom inherited from the Chinese, who brought these dishes to Thailand. Noodle soups are exclusively eaten with chopsticks, and fried noodles are eaten either with chopsticks or with a fork and spoon.

TABLE MANNERS

THE ELDEST GETS THINGS UNDERWAY

When you are having a meal with your family or colleagues, you must wait until the eldest or the person with the highest social rank starts to help themselves before beginning to serve yourself. Respect for one's elders is an absolute must. Among friends, the atmosphere is more relaxed, and this unspoken rule does not apply.

DO NOT FILL YOUR PLATE

Dishes served at the table are shared among all guests. Help yourself to a small amount of one or two dishes, and eat what is on your plate before taking more. Filling your plate as though you were at an all-you-can-eat buffet is rude and gives the impression that you are eating without concern for others.

EAT SLOWLY

Do not throw yourself onto your food, as this also gives the impression that you are eating without concern for other guests. Take the time to interact with your companions and create a friendly atmosphere.

DO NOT STAB FOOD WITH YOUR FORK

Hold your spoon in your right hand, and use it to bring food to your mouth. Use your fork to push food into your spoon or to cut any pieces that may be too big.

DO NOT BLOW YOUR NOSE AT THE TABLE

Do this on your way to the bathroom, or wipe your nose discreetly with a tissue.

LEAVE A LITTLE FOOD IN THE DISHES AND ON YOUR PLATE

Show your guests that you have had enough by leaving a little food behind. Finish your rice, though!

A FEW RULES FOR CHOPSTICKS

- Do not stick your chopsticks in the rice bowl, as this is reminiscent of the incense sticks used to mourn the dead.
- Do not play with your chopsticks or point them at anyone.
- Do not cross your chopsticks — it is bad luck.

COOKING TECHNIQUES

OVER A FIRE

Boiling (*tom*; ต้ม): This is the traditional cooking method to prepare soups in earthenware pots.

Simmering (*toun*; ตุ๋น): This method is used to cook meat stews and curries.

OVER CHARCOAL

Thai cuisine relies heavily on traditional charcoal grilling. There is a wide variety of terms for the different methods of grilling food.

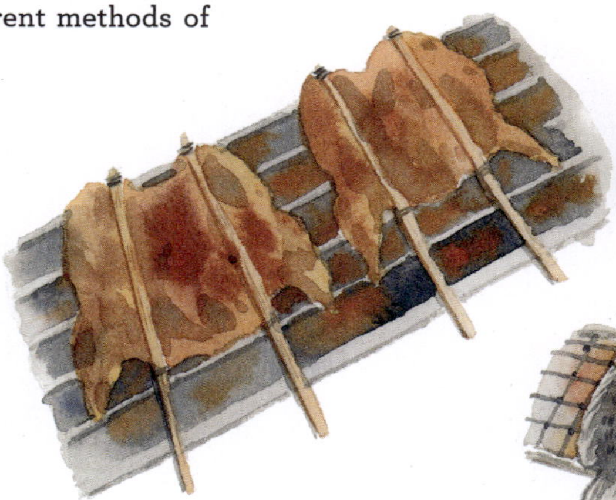

Roasting (*yang*; ย่าง)

Grilling skewers (*ping*; ปิ้ง)

Grilling fish (*pla pao*, meaning "to burn"; ปลาเผา)

Grilling food wrapped in banana leaves (*ep*; แอ๊บ)

Grilling in bamboo, like for *khao lam* (ข้าวหลาม)

WITH STEAM

Cooking with steam (*neung*; นึ่ง): Sticky rice, fish, finger foods, steamed buns and jelly desserts can all be cooked in a basket over a pot of steamy water.

IN A WOK

Stir-frying and deep-frying in a wok descended directly from Chinese immigrants. Today, they are an integral part of Thai cuisine.

Stir-frying (*pad*; ผัด): This cooking method is very fast and allows food to be seared while still retaining a nice texture. Vegetables, meats, noodles and rice can all be stir-fried.

Deep-frying (*thod;* ทอด): Thais are fond of deep-frying, particularly for snacks such as fried chicken, banana fritters and curry fritters. Meats, fish and even noodles can be deep-fried.

Yam (ยำ): This term, which translates to "mixture," often refers to salads. However, it can also refer to other dishes that have a particular blend of flavors (tangy, salty and spicy), such as *tom yam* soup.

BREAKFAST

The sun rises early in Thailand, and with it comes sweltering heat, so people tend to start their day at dawn. Breakfast stalls usually open at six in the morning and close at nine, or earlier if they have sold out. It is customary to eat breakfast on the go outside, on the way to work or school. Breakfast can also be eaten at home: You buy some takeout at the corner or finish off the leftovers from the previous evening's meal. Whatever the case, breakfast tends to be a savory meal made up of dishes that are as likely to be eaten for lunch or dinner.

However, a few dishes are especially popular for morning meals, although these too can be eaten later in the day. They include rice porridge (*jok*; โจ๊ก), fritters (*patonko*; ปาท่องโก๋), fried chicken (*kai thod*; ไก่ทอด), grilled pork skewers with sticky rice (*khao niew moo ping*; ข้าวเหนียวหมูปิ้ง) and chicken with rice (*khao man kai*; ข้าวมันไก่). These specialties are invariably prepared in advance (rather than being cooked to order), so they can be served quickly. They are also easy to eat. However, if you have more time and can sit down, you can order any number of dishes from street stalls.

BREAKFAST SOUPS

Rice porridge (*jok*; โจ๊ก) served with pork meatballs, a poached or soft-boiled egg and finely minced ginger and scallion is the dish most frequently associated with breakfast in Thailand. It is particularly popular with young children.

Khao tom (ข้าวต้ม) is a rice soup made from leftover cooked rice along with broth and the toppings of your choice (popular options include seafood, vegetables and ground pork). This dish is much simpler to prepare than *jok*, so it is more often cooked at home, as is the omelet and rice dish *khao khai jiew*.

Tom luad moo (ต้มเลือดหมู) is a soup made of pork offal and coagulated pork blood and is usually served with rice. It is one of the Thais' favorite breakfast soups.

OTHER BREAKFAST SPECIALITIES

Patonko fritters (ปาท่องโก๋) are particularly popular for breakfast. They are served with soy milk (*nam tao hoo*; น้ำเต้าหู้) and often only sold in the morning.

Grilled pork skewers with sticky rice (*khao niew moo ping*; ข้าวเหนียวหมูปิ้ง) are another breakfast staple, although they are readily eaten at any time of day.

There are also dishes that are particular to specific regions. For example, Isan's Laotian influences and French colonial heritage have popularized fried eggs accompanied with various pork sides (a bologna-like sausage, ground pork, cured pork, sausages) and a baguette. This dish is called *khai krata* (ไข่กระทะ), which literally means "eggs served in the pan."

BREAKFAST BEVERAGES

The classic breakfast beverages are coffee and *boran* tea, served hot or iced. *Oliang* coffee is the traditional Thai coffee.

LUNCH

Thais take their lunch break around midday, usually outside. It is a fairly quick, light meal before returning to work. It is also typically a plated dish that is not shared (*ahan jan diew*; อาหารจานเดียว): rice and a side, fried rice or noodles, noodle soup.

Noodle soup
Kouay tiew
ก๋วยเตี๋ยว

Stir-fried pork
Khao pad moo
ข้าวผัด

Stir-fried shrimp with basil
Pad kaprao kung
ผัดกะเพรากุ้ง

Fleeing the sweltering midday heat,
Thais like to take refuge in air-conditioned
restaurants and food courts for lunch.

DINNER

The sun sets early in Thailand. It is not uncommon for locals to dine on the go after work around six o'clock or to join friends for a drink on the way home. At home, families usually dine between six and seven. They prepare a balanced meal with a variety of dishes, some homemade and others picked up on the way home. Dinner is the most important meal of the day and is when families get together to chat and catch up.

KHAP KHAO: A MEAL BASED AROUND RICE

A typical evening meal consists of rice and three to five different dishes presented in the center of the table and shared by the whole family. This type of meal is called *khap khao*, which means "with rice." The more people there are around the table, the more dishes are served. The food is varied, and there are always dishes suited to young children, who generally do not eat spicy food. There is always a soup or a curry and a *nam prik* platter along with one or more stir-fries (with vegetables and with or without meat). A piece of fish or some meat and salads eventually make it to the table.

Tom jeud tao hoo moo sab soup (ต้มจืดเต้าหู้หมูสับ) is a must for family dinners, especially when there are children present. Its name literally means "bland tofu and ground pork soup." It is aptly named, totally lacking spices and chili. This clear broth and pork meatball soup topped with silken tofu and cabbage is much loved by Thais, despite its rather unappetizing name.

Water spinach stir-fry (*pad pak boong*; ผัดผักบุ้ง) is very quick and easy to prepare. It is another must-have dish for family dinners.

Nam prik pla tu (น้ำพริกปลาทู) is an easy-to-prepare, nutritious condiment dish made with fish and fresh vegetables. It is often served at dinner.

Kaeng som pak ruam kung sod (แกงส้มผักรวมกุ้งสด) is a tangy curry made with tamarind juice, various vegetables and shrimp. It is also easy to make and is one of the most popular curries at the dinner table.

Yam are Thai "salads," but they do not necessarily consist of raw vegetables. The name refers to a dressing similar to vinaigrette that is typically tangy, salty and spicy. Vegetables, under-ripe fruits, a variety of meats and fish or, as pictured here, noodles can all be included. The rice vermicelli salad *yam woon sen* (ยำวุ้นเส้น), garnished with ground pork, seafood or pork bologna, is very easy to prepare and is often on the evening menu.

SNACKS

Thais snack all day long, often more out of indulgence than hunger. As a result, both sweet and savory snacks can be bought on the street from early morning until late at night. Noodle stalls are even open until the middle of the night to cater to night owls. Yes, in Thailand, a bowl of noodle soup can absolutely be a snack!

POPULAR SNACKS

Karipap, khanom krok and *khanom buang* are popular snacks all over the country. Each comes in a savory version and a sweet one, to suit every palate and every snack time.

Karipap (กะหรี่ปั๊บ)
This dish's name is derived from the English "curry puff." They are deep-fried fritters with a wide variety of fillings: curried chicken and potatoes, vegetables, egg, fish, fruit ... They can be found in many other South Asian countries, from India to Malaysia.

Kanom buang (ขนมเบื้อง)
These are small pancakes filled with meringue and a sweet or savory filling. The sweet one, *foithong,* is a duck egg yolk candied in sugar syrup. The savory filling is made with grated coconut meat and dried shrimp.

Kanom krok (ขนมครก)
These little bites are named after the pan in which they are cooked, which has many round indentations, similar in shape to a mortar (*krok*). These coconut milk snacks are reminiscent of flan. Crisp on the outside and soft on the inside, they can be filled with corn, chopped scallions or mung beans.

IT'S HAPPY HOUR!

Thais love to have fun. Evening is a special time to get together with colleagues or friends for a friendly drink! These gatherings usually take place outdoors, in a bar or restaurant, and the boundaries are often blurred in a country where you would not think of serving drinks without food! Beers are usually served with light snacks to nibble on, such as salads, fried foods or grilled meats.

MARKETS

Thailand has a real market culture, known as *talad* (ตลาด). You can find them in every town, big or small, all over the country. There are the morning food markets, where you buy raw ingredients to be cooked. There are also markets open in the afternoon and early evening where you can eat or buy takeout food. Finally, there are the so-called "night markets," which are open late into the night and offer live music and other entertainment, shopping and, of course, food. Thailand is a country where you can really enjoy the nightlife, after the sun has set and the heat starts to dissipate, even if it is just to go for a stroll and hang out.

NIGHT MARKETS

The atmosphere at night markets is one of relaxation, shopping and fun. It is not uncommon to find musicians and children's games among the stalls selling drinks, food and all manner of goods (clothes, toys, leather goods, costume jewelry, etc.). Outside the capital, these markets are often held once a week or at weekends. In tourist towns, some are open every night.

THE KHLONG TOEI MARKET

Located in Bangkok, Khlong Toei is the country's largest food market, covering some 37 acres (15 ha)! It is alive day and night, with stalls open 24 hours a day. It is the supply hub for all of the capital's restaurants and street vendors.

RESTAURANTS

ETIQUETTE RULES

When dining out, certain unspoken rules prevail:

- We eat a *khap khao*, that is, a meal with rice, and all of the dishes are placed in the center of the table and shared. Dishes continue to be served as the meal progresses, so there is no need to wait until everything is on the table to start eating.
- It is customary for the oldest person at the table to place the order. Guests can let their elder know if they have a particular craving, but they will not order directly from the server.
- In a professional setting, whoever occupies the highest social position places the order and pays the bill. In any case, everyone waits for the elders to invite them to start the meal or to begin eating themselves.
- Thais are considerate: Do not be surprised if they put the most appetizing morsel on your plate. Just accept this kind and thoughtful gesture.
- Things are more relaxed between friends and colleagues, both when ordering and when settling the bill. But if someone decides to pay the bill, it is impolite to insist on contributing.

HOW DO I ORDER IN A RESTAURANT?

The polite formulas *ka* (ค่ะ) for women and *krap* (ครับ) for men are consistently added at the end of sentences.

Excuse me.
Ko thod ka/krap.
ขอโทษค่ะ/ครับ

Server, please
(if it is someone younger than you).
Nong ka/krap.
น้องคะ/ครับ

Server, please
(if they are the same age as you or older).
Pi ka/krap.
พี่คะ/ครับ

Do you have a menu in English, please?
Mi menu phasa angkrit mai ka/krap.
มีเมนูภาษาอังกฤษไหมคะ/ครับ

May I order?
Sang ahan noy ka/krap.
สั่งอาหารหน่อยค่ะ/ครับ

I would like ...
Ao ... ka/krap.
เอา ... ค่ะ/ครับ

I will have the *pad thai*, please.
Ao pad thai ka/krap.
เอาผัดไทยค่ะ/ครับ

No chili, please.
Mai sai prik.
ไม่ใส่พริก

No peanuts, please.
Mai sai tua.
ไม่ใส่ถั่ว

No egg, please.
Mai sai khai.
ไม่ใส่ไข่

I am allergic to ...
Pe ...
แพ้ ...

I am vegetarian.
Kin je.
กินเจ

Where is the restroom, please?
Hong nam you nay ka/krap.
ห้องน้ำอยู่ไหนคะ/ครับ

May I please have the bill?
Check bin ka/krap.
เช็คบิลล์ค่ะ/ครับ

FOODS WRAPPED IN LEAVES

Thailand's lush natural environment offers a wealth of resources that have been harvested by the local population for centuries. Just think of the bamboo used to build rafts, huts and furniture — and to cook rice. Young bamboo shoots are even eaten. Tree and plant leaves are another abundantly available raw material. The traditional use of leaves for wrapping or preparing certain dishes is still widely practiced today.

PANDAN LEAVES

Pandan leaves (*bai teuille*; ใบเตย) have an unmistakable aroma. They are often used in desserts, and they can also be used to wrap certain dishes, such *kai hor bai teuille* (ไก่ห่อใบเตย), which is a marinated and fried chicken dish.

Mieng kham (เมี่ยงคำ)
This popular traditional snack, whose name literally means "bite wrapped in a leaf," is also found in Laos. In Thailand, the various fillings (scallion, chili, dried shrimp, toasted shredded coconut, peanuts, lime, ginger) are accompanied by a sweet and salty sauce. It is all placed in the center of a leaf from which it is eaten. Traditionally, leaves from the coral bean tree (*bai thong lang*; ใบทองหลาง) were used, but today betel leaves (*bai chaplu*; ใบชะพลู) are much more common. Chinese broccoli leaves are sometimes used, and a more elaborate version features lotus petals.

BANANA LEAVES

Being both flexible and heat-resistant, banana leaves have many uses in the kitchen. They can be used as a side plate or as a wrapping in which to carry food. They can also be used as a wrapping in which to cook food, whether grilled over an open fire, steamed or even boiled. Unlike other leaves, banana leaves do not give off an odor that can alter foods' flavors. There is a wide variety of snacks wrapped in banana leaves, often consisting of a sticky rice base and a filling.

Khao tom mad (ข้าวต้มมัด)
This is a popular snack of sticky rice cooked in coconut milk and topped with banana and black soybeans. It is steamed in a banana leaf. It can also be topped with taro or sweet potato.

Khanom sai sai (ขนมใส่ไส้)
This is an ancient traditional snack: A paste of sticky rice flour flavored with pandan is stuffed with shredded coconut and cooked in a palm sugar syrup. The whole thing is then wrapped in banana leaves and coconut before being steamed.

Hor mok (ห่อหมก)
This specialty of Khmer origin is a red curry custard wrapped in banana leaves and then steamed. It is commonly made with fish (*hor mok pla*; ห่อหมกปลา) or seafood (*hor mok talay*; ห่อหมกทะเล).

Aeb pla (แอ๊บปลา)
This northern specialty is a curried fish preparation grilled inside a wrapping of banana leaves. It is also available with pork (*aeb moo*; แอบหม).

JUNGLE FOOD

Thailand has a deep-rooted tradition of so-called "jungle food" (*ahan pa*; อาหารป่า). Some meats are hunted, while others are farmed. You will find game meats such as boar, venison and pheasant and meats that are less common in the West: snakes, rice rats, frogs and ant and worm larvae. Some of these, like frogs and rats, are an inexpensive source of food in the poorest, most remote regions. Others, like red ant larvae, are highly prized and quite expensive.

Grilled rice rats are a popular dish in Isan, in northeastern Thailand.

Jungle food is an ancient culinary tradition that has endured, particularly in rural areas. Today, there are specialty restaurants as well as establishments that offer off-menu dishes when they receive special orders. More traditional meats and fish, such as chicken and pork, are also used but prepared with an abundance of forest herbs and lots of chili.

A FEW SPECIALTIES

Red ant larvae omelet
Khai jiew sai khai mod deng
ไข่เจียวไข่มดแดง

Boar and pineapple stem stir-fry
Pad moo pa juk sapparod
ผัดหมูป่าจุกสับปะรด

Pheasant and basil stir-fry
Kra prao nok pa
กะเพรานกป่า

Frog stir-fry
Pad pet kop
ผัดเผ็ดกบ

ไทย

REGIONAL CUISINES

The Thailand we know today is a very young country. For centuries, kingdoms with very different borders succeeded one another. First there was the Sukhothai Kingdom, which occupied a long territory stretching from present-day Laos to northern Malaysia. It is considered to be the first country of the Thai people. It was followed by the Ayutthaya Kingdom, which was bordered to the north by another independent kingdom, Lanna. The Isan region to the northeast and present-day Laos belonged to the Kingdom of Lan Xang for centuries, while the far south was part of the Pattani Kingdom, which was caught between Siam and Malaysia. At the height of its power in the 18th century, Thailand, then known as the Kingdom of Siam, ruled over a large part of Southeast Asia, including present-day Laos and Cambodia. Europe's colonial ambitions in the early 20th century finally shaped the borders of present-day Thailand.

These ancient kingdoms have all disappeared, but the gastronomic and cultural links they shared are still very much alive among the people of Thailand and their neighbors. Today, the diversity and richness of Thai cuisine is based on four major regions with very different traditions, climates and terrains.

NORTHERN CUISINE

AN ETHNIC CROSSROADS

With its richly diverse population, this region has been influenced as much by Burma and Laos, with whom it shares a common history, as by waves of Chinese immigrants. You will find dishes with Burmese, Chinese and Laotian touches. Northern Thailand encompassed the Lanna Kingdom from the 13th century to the end of the 19th century. The region is an important crossroads, and its local cuisine was shaped by a diversity of caravanners, particularly the spices they brought with them.

THE FLAVORS OF THE NORTH

The Lanna region encompasses plains and mountains and is a long way from the sea. The climate can be cool, so produce is often more nourishing than in the rest of the country. The most popular meats come from farmed animals, such as chicken and beef, and pork is the star of the plate! Spices acquired from Persian traders are an integral part of the cuisine, as are vegetables and herbs from the surrounding forests. The predominate flavors are salty, tangy, herbaceous and earthy, along with grilled and smoky notes. Overall, the cuisine is moderately spicy and sweet compared to the rest of the country. Coconut milk is rarely used, as coconut palms are not native to the region.

Along the mountain slopes, local populations cultivate the country's only terraced rice paddies. Lanna (ล้านนา) actually means "Kingdom of Countless Rice Paddies."

Jin som mok (จิ้นส้มหมก), or *naem moo* (แหนมหมู) in Isan, is an acidic fermented pork sausage that is popular in the northern regions bordering Laos.

Tua nao (ถั่วเน่า) is a distinctive ingredient of northern Thailand and is also found in Burmese Shan cuisine. It is a dried and fermented soybean patty that is roasted before being ground to a powder. It is used to add depth to dishes.

KHANTOK (ขันโตก): THE TRADITIONAL MENU

The traditional northern menu, called *khantok*, also refers to the platter on which it is served. It consists of sticky rice and several accompanying dishes, including ...

Sai oua (ไส้อั่ว): These sausages are flavored with curry, lemongrass and Kaffir lime leaves.

Laab muang (ลาบเมือง): This salad of raw ground meat and offal (traditionally buffalo) is flavored with a variety of spices and seasoned with blood and bile. It is a much-loved regional delicacy and a celebratory dish. When cooked, it is called *laab khua* (ลาบคั่ว).

Nam prik (น้ำพริก): There are many possible accompaniments to *nam prik*. The most popular are *nam prik ong* (น้ำพริกอ่อง), which is made with ground pork and roasted tomatoes, and *nam prik num*(น้ำพริกหนุ่ม), which is made with roasted green chilies.

A soup or curry, such as the popular *hung ley curry* (แกงฮังเล), featuring pork belly braised with spices reminiscent of Burmese flavors, is also usually served as part of a *khantok*.

A platter of fresh herbs and raw or boiled vegetables, as well as *kap moo* (แคปหมู), which are deep-fried pork rind crackers, rounds out the meal.

OTHER POPULAR DISHES

Khanom jin nam ngeo (ขนมจีนน้ำเงี้ยว): This age-old icon from the Lanna Kingdom is served during celebrations. It is a stew influenced by Burmese cuisine, made with tomatoes, fermented soybean paste, cubes of coagulated pork or chicken blood, ground pork or beef and *kapok dok ngeo* flowers. It is served with *khanom jin* (fermented rice vermicelli).

Jackfruit curry (*kaeng khanun*; แกงขนุน): As the name suggests, this thin, liquid curry is made with unripe jackfruit. This specialty is often served at weddings and celebrations. *Nun* means "support" in Thai, so jackfruit is considered to be a good omen.

Cabbage soup (*jor pak kad*; จอผักกาด): This is a specialty often served at northern tables and reflects Chinese influences. It is a delicious soup made of cabbage and pork ribs that is seasoned with tangy tamarind.

HUNG LEY CURRY (แกงฮังเล)

Hung ley curry is an extremely popular northern dish that dates back to the Burmese occupation of the region. Made with pork belly, ginger and pickled garlic, it is both tangy and richly spiced but not very hot.

Yield: 4 to 6 servings
Prep time: 1 hour + 20 minutes
Marinating time: at least 30 minutes
Cook time: 1 hour

CURRY PASTE

- 7 dried long chilies, roasted, deseeded and rehydrated
- 1 tsp. (5 ml) salt
- 2 stalks lemongrass, tender parts only, chopped
- 1-inch (3 cm) piece fresh galangal, chopped
- 1-inch (3 cm) piece fresh ginger, peeled and chopped
- 1-inch (3 cm) piece fresh turmeric, peeled and chopped
- 1 tbsp. (15 ml) coriander seeds, toasted
- 2 tsp. (10 ml) cumin seeds, toasted
- 3 whole star anise, toasted
- 5 whole cloves, toasted
- ¾-inch (2 cm) cinnamon stick, toasted
- 2 Thai cardamom pods, seeds only, toasted
- 10 cloves garlic
- 3 shallots, grilled
- 1 tbsp. (15 ml) shrimp paste

OTHER INGREDIENTS

- 10 ounces (300 g) pork belly
- 10 ounces (300 g) pork shoulder
- 4 ounces (125 g) fresh ginger (about ½ cup peeled and minced)
- 3 tbsp. (45 ml) peanuts
- 2 tbsp. (30 ml) lard or neutral vegetable oil
- 1¼ cups (300 ml) pork stock or water
- 2 tbsp. (30 ml) palm sugar
- 3 tbsp. (45 ml) tamarind paste
- 4 ounces (125 g) pickled garlic (about 15 to 20 cloves)
- 2 tbsp. (30 ml) fish sauce

1. Prepare the curry paste using a mortar and pestle, incorporating the ingredients in the order listed.
2. Chop the pork belly and shoulder into ¾-inch (2 cm) pieces and combine with the curry paste. Let marinate for 30 minutes.
3. Meanwhile, peel and mince the additional ginger and roast the peanuts in a dry pan.
4. Add the lard to a wok or Dutch oven and brown the pork on all sides for a few minutes over medium heat.
5. Add the stock and simmer over low heat for 50 minutes, until the pork is tender.
6. Add the prepared ginger and peanuts together with the palm sugar, tamarind paste, pickled garlic and fish sauce. Let simmer for a further 10 minutes.
7. Adjust the seasoning if desired, and serve with sticky rice. This curry is best enjoyed the same day it is prepared.

KHAO SOI (ข้าวซอย)

The most iconic dish of the north, *khao soi* noodle soup is a testament to the Chin Haw, who migrated from China. There is also a Burmese version of this soup.

Yield: 4 servings
Prep time: 45 minutes + 15 minutes
Cook time: 50 minutes to 1 hour

CURRY PASTE

- 5 dried long red chilies, roasted, deseeded and rehydrated
- 1 tsp. (5 ml) salt
- 1 tsp. (5 ml) coriander seeds, toasted
- ½ tsp. (2 ml) cumin seeds, toasted
- 1 tsp. (5 ml) Kaffir lime zest
- 1- to 1½-inch (3–4 cm) piece fresh ginger, peeled and chopped
- 2-inch (6 cm) piece fresh turmeric, peeled and chopped
- 3 cilantro roots or 2 tbsp. (30 ml) thinly sliced cilantro stems
- 2 shallots, chopped
- 3 cloves garlic

OTHER INGREDIENTS

- 14 ounces (400 g) fresh egg noodles
- 4 to 6 chicken drumsticks
- 3 tbsp. + ¾ cup (45 ml + 175 ml) neutral oil
- 3¼ cups (800 ml) coconut milk
- 1 tbsp. (15 ml) palm sugar
- 2 tbsp. (30 ml) light soy sauce
- 1 tsp. (5 ml) dark soy sauce
- 1 tbsp. (15 ml) fish sauce
- A few sprigs of fresh cilantro, thinly sliced
- 2 shallots, thinly sliced
- ½ lime, quartered
- *Pak kad dong* (pickled mustard greens)

1 Prepare the curry paste using a mortar and pestle, incorporating the ingredients in the order listed.

2 Heat 1 tbsp. (15 ml) oil in a frying pan over high heat and brown the chicken drumsticks, skin side down. Set aside.

3 Heat a little oil in a large saucepan or Dutch oven over medium heat. Add a bit of coconut cream (the solids from a can of coconut milk) and the curry paste, and stir-fry. Once the moisture has evaporated and the oil begins to separate, add the rest of the coconut milk and stir to combine.

4 Add the chicken, palm sugar and sauces. Let simmer for 30 to 40 minutes.

5 Heat ¾ cups (200 ml) oil in a wok or saucepan and fry a quarter of the noodles, leaving them untangled, in their "nest." Turn them over so they brown evenly, and then place them on paper towels to drain.

6 Cook the remaining noodles in a pot of boiling water for 2 to 3 minutes. Rinse the boiled noodles in cold water to stop the cooking.

7 Divide the boiled noodles and chicken among 4 large bowls. Cover generously with curry sauce, and then top with fried noodles, cilantro, shallots, a lime wedge and mustard greens.

NORTHEASTERN CUISINE

ISAN AND LAOS: A FAMILY HISTORY

Isan (อีสาน) refers to the northeastern region of Thailand, bordering Laos. The region long belonged to the ancient Kingdom of Lan Xang (present-day Laos). It only became part of the Kingdom of Siam (Thailand's former name) in 1935, and the area is still mainly populated by people of Laotian descent. The population has preserved a dialect closer to Laotian than to Thai, as well as Laos's centuries-old gastronomic tradition based on the iconic green papaya salad and sticky rice. Thailand's border with Laos is bound by the Mekong River, whose tributaries irrigate the entire region.

Isan is an agricultural area known as Thailand's "rice basket," but poverty is rampant. The lack of jobs and prospects have driven many inhabitants to resettle throughout the country. They have taken their culinary traditions with them, and Isan dishes with Laotian roots are now being served from small stalls all over the country. Isan cuisine is very popular with tourists and contributes greatly to the reputation of Thai gastronomy.

THE FLAVORS OF THE NORTHEAST

Isan cuisine is simple peasant fare, easily prepared in a region where most work in fields. It is also one of the spiciest in the country, but it does not use foreign spices, favoring herbs and aromatic plants that are locally available in abundance. Much of the food comes from the surrounding countryside. The people of Isan eat river fish, farmed animals (pork, chicken and beef on special occasions) and forage (frogs, rice rats and insects such as locusts, ants and ant larvae). The flavors are intense, salty, tangy and very spicy. Seasonings such as fermented fish sauces (*pla ra*; ปลาร้า) and buffalo bile (*nam dii*; น้ำดี) and digestive juices (*nam phia*; น้ำเพี้ย), with their strong bitterness, can scare off city dwellers' more delicate palates.

BAMBOO: AN ISAN SPECIALTY

Bamboo grows in abundance in the wilderness of Isan's forests. It is also a natural resource with many uses. The wood is used in construction and to manufacture domestic objects (carpets, woven baskets, etc.), while the young shoots are eaten in a wide variety of dishes.

In curry
Kaeng nor mai bai yanang
แกงหน่อไม้ใบย่านาง

In salads
Sup nor mai
ซุปหน่อไม้

Wrapped in leaves and steamed
Mok nor mai
หมกหน่อไม้

Kratip: a woven bamboo basket for storing sticky rice.

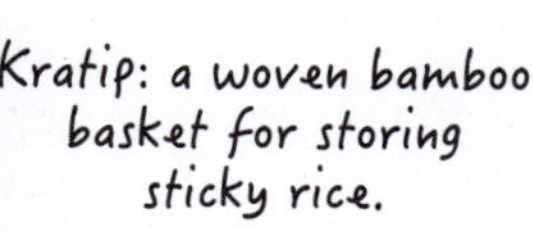

Bamboo can also be used to carry and cook food, such as for *khao lam* (ข้าวหลาม), a sweet snack cooked over coals. It is made from sweet sticky rice, coconut milk and occasionally mung beans.

A TRADITIONAL MEAL IN ISAN

A traditional Isan meal consists of sticky rice in woven bamboo baskets, called *kratip*, and a variety of dishes. The following are the must-haves.

SOM TAM (ส้มตำ)

This green papaya salad is spicy, salty and tangy. It is the hallmark of northeastern cuisine. Several variations exist, such as *tam thai*, the milder version made with peanuts and dried shrimp; *tam lao* (or *tam pla ra*), with its strong flavor of fermented *pla ra* fish sauce; and *tam poo*, which is made with salted freshwater crab and fish sauce.

LAAB (ลาบ)

This salad of ground meat and fresh herbs is served warm. It is the region's other signature dish. At once spicy, salty and tangy, a *laab* can be made with a variety of meats, such as pork, chicken, duck or beef, or even fish or mushrooms. It is topped with *khao khua*, a toasted rice powder that gives it a delicious roasted aroma.

NAM TOK (น้ำตก)

This salad is similar to *laab* in seasoning, but it is made with slices of marinated and grilled meat. The name of the dish means "waterfall" and refers to the cooking method, which allows the meat juices to drop through the barbecue grill, reminiscent of a waterfall.

KAI YANG (ไก่ย่าง) AND *MOO YANG* (หมูย่าง)

These dishes feature chicken or pork that is marinated, barbecued and served with tamarind *nam jim jeow* sauce. The meat is lightly caramelized as it cooks. These popular dishes bring a gourmet touch of sweetness to the table.

A jar used to ferment *pla ra* fish sauce (ปลาร้า).

KAENG OM (แกงอ่อม)

This herbaceous curry is closer to a soup than a traditional curry. The curry paste is quite simple, made with fresh chilies, aromatic herbs, garlic and shallots. You then add the protein of your choice (chicken, pork or fish) along with a selection of vegetables and cover everything with water, not forgetting the *pla ra* fish sauce.

JEOW (แจ่ว)

These are spicy dips similar to the ubiquitous *nam prik* eaten elsewhere in Thailand. Among the most popular are *jeow mak len*, made with tomato, and *jeow mak khua*, made with eggplant. Fresh or boiled vegetables and *kap moo* (fried pork rind crackers) are served alongside.

OTHER SPECIALTIES

KHAO JI (ข้าวจี่)

This street snack makes the most of leftover rice. It consists of a skewer of small sticky rice cakes that are soaked in egg and then barbecued. They are crispy on the outside and soft on the inside!

SAI KROK ISAN (ไส้กรอกอีสาน)

A combination of fermented pork sausages, sticky rice and fresh herbs, this grilled dish is enjoyed at any time of day but particularly as a snack before dinner. It is traditionally served with crunchy fresh vegetables, such as cabbage, and a spicy sauce.

SOM TAM THAI (ส้มตำไทย)

This spicy green papaya salad is an icon of northeastern cuisine. Many variations exist, but *som tam thai* is the sweetest and most popular version.

Yield: 2 servings
Prep time: 20 minutes

- 1 tbsp. (15 ml) small dried shrimp
- 2 cloves garlic
- 1 to 10 Thai chilies
- 1 tbsp. (15 ml) tamarind pulp
- 1½ tbsp. (22 ml) palm sugar
- 3 tbsp. (45 ml) fish sauce
- 2 tbsp. (30 ml) lime juice
- 8 cherry tomatoes
- ½ green papaya
- 8-inch (20 cm) length of long bean or 6 green beans
- 2 tbsp. (30 ml) unsalted roasted peanuts

1. Peel and grate the green papaya. Chop the palm sugar and halve the tomatoes. Slice the beans into ¾-inch (2 cm) lengths.
2. Vigorously crush the dried shrimp, garlic, chilies and tamarind pulp with a mortar and pestle.
3. Add the palm sugar, fish sauce, lime juice, half the tomato halves and a small handful of papaya. Give the mixture a few taps with the pestle to release the tomatoes' juices and dissolve the sugar.
4. Add the remaining papaya and tomatoes along with the beans and peanuts. Mash the mixture for 1 minute, alternating between the pestle and a spoon: The objective is a uniform mixture that retains the vegetables' crunchiness.
5. Adjust the seasoning if desired: more lemon for acidity, more fish sauce for saltiness and more sugar for sweetness.

LAAP MOO (ลาบหมู)

Laab refers to the action of grinding meat and *moo* to pork. This version of *laab* is very popular, but it can be made with any other meat.

Yield: 4 servings
Prep time: 10 minutes
Cook time: 5 minutes

- 21 ounces (600 g) lean ground pork
- ¼ cup (60 ml) uncooked sticky rice
- 2 shallots
- 4 scallions
- 1 bunch fresh mint
- 1 small bunch fresh cilantro
- 1 tbsp. (15 ml) chili flakes
- ¼ cup (60 ml) lime juice
- ¼ cup (60 ml) fish sauce

1. Prepare *khao khua* by toasting the grains of sticky rice in a dry frying pan until they are golden-brown and then blending them to a powder.
2. Thinly slice the shallots and scallions. Roughly chop the mint and cilantro leaves.
3. Bring a pot of water to a simmer and cook the pork, breaking it up as it cooks to ensure it has a nice ground-meat consistency.
4. Combine the remaining ingredients except for the mint and cilantro with the meat.
5. This dish is best served at room temperature. Leave the meat to cool, and then add the herbs and serve with sticky rice.

CENTRAL CUISINE

THE COUNTRY'S SIGNATURE CUISINE

The cuisine of central Thailand first evokes Ayutthaya, the ancient capital of Siam. Ayutthaya was nicknamed the "Venice of the Orient," a moniker that was passed to Bangkok, the capital built on the waters of the Chao Phraya River. Bangkok is famous for its freshwater fish, river prawns and iconic street food.

The gastronomy of central Thailand features many of the country's world-renowned dishes, such as *pad thai*, green curry, red curry, *massaman* curry, *tom yam kung* soup and *tom kha kai* soup. It is a refined and complex cuisine, with some dishes descended from royal kitchens. It is also a diverse cuisine that evolved over centuries, encompassing the traditions of the early Mon people and the defeated Khmer as well as waves of Chinese, Persian, Indian, Malay and Portuguese migrants, to name but a few. It is a veritable historical melting pot. You would have to explore all these influences to truly understand the region's gastronomy! Central Thailand is also defined by its geography and irrigated plains, which are ideal for growing the jasmine rice that is so very popular in the region.

THE FLAVORS OF CENTRAL THAILAND

The region's cuisine is distinguished by its essential aromatic herbs (galangal, lemongrass, Kaffir lime leaves, holy basil and sweet Thai basil), its curries sweetened with palm sugar and coconut milk that are less spicy than in the south and northeast, and its seasonings (*nam pla* and *kapi*). Tables are laid with a profusion of meat, fish, seafood and vegetable dishes served as appetizers, salads, soups and curries that are simmered, grilled or stir-fried. For special occasions, platters are beautifully decorated with carved vegetables, testifying to the richness of the region's culinary repertoire.

SPECIALTIES INHERITED FROM THE MONS

The Mons were the first people to populate the Chao Phraya Basin. Central Thailand's gastronomy boasts some of the great classics inherited from this people.

Khao kluk kapi

Khanom jin nam prik

Khanom jin sao nam

Khao kluk kapi (ข้าวคลุกกะปิ) is a complete dish made with the two great staples of Thai cuisine: rice and shrimp paste (*kapi*). The age-old fermentation process used to produce *kapi* preserves this important protein, the most abundant in the Chao Phraya Basin, for long-term storage. The rice is served with an assortment of toppings: acacia leaf omelet, raw vegetables, green mango, Chinese sausages, braised pork, dried shrimp and fresh or roasted chilies.

Khanom jin (ขนมจีน) refers to fermented rice vermicelli that is served with curries. It varies from region to region, and Thailand's central region boasts several variations of *khanom jin*.

One example is the classic *khanom jin nam prik* (ขนมจีนน้ำพริก), a creamy, sweet and tangy coconut curry. It is created with a chili and shrimp paste, mung bean seeds and roasted peanuts, and it is paired with both raw vegetables and tempura vegetables.

Another popular variant is *khanom jin sao nam* (ขนมจีนซาวน้ำ). The noodles are served with dried shrimp powder, young coconut meat, minced young ginger, minced garlic, pineapple, fish balls, hard-boiled eggs and sweetened coconut milk.

THE CHINESE INFLUENCE IN BANGKOK

Thai society has been strongly influenced by the waves of Chinese migrants who have been settling in the region since the 13th century. Chinese immigration, particularly from the Chaozhou region (or *Teochew* in Thai), was so significant from the end of the 18th century that by the beginning of the 20th century, 50% of Bangkok's residents were of Chinese heritage!

In terms of gastronomy, the Chinese influence is immense, whether through the introduction of cooking techniques (stir-frying in a wok, deep-frying and steaming) or ingredients indispensable to modern Thai cuisine (such as noodles and soy sauce). There are countless Chinese-Thai dishes, so much so that they make up the majority of the offerings at the capital's street food stalls.

STIR-FRIED NOODLES

Pad see ew (ผัดซีอิ๊ว)
Pad ki mao (ผัดขี้เมา)
Mi krob (หมี่กรอบ)

PORK

Khao ka moo (ข้าวขาหมู): braised pork
Moo palo (หมูพะโล้): five-spice pork
Moo dang (หมูแดง): barbecue pork
Moo krob (หมูกรอบ): crispy pork

NOODLE SOUPS

Kouay jap (กวยจั๊บ)
Kouay tiew rua (ก๋วยเตี๋ยวเรือ)
Ba mi (บะหมี่)

SNACKS

Kanom jib (ขนมจีบ): steamed bites
Salapao (ซาลาเปา): stuffed buns
Patongo (ปาท่องโก๋): fritters
Hoi thod (หอยทอด): oyster omelet

TOM YAM KUNG (ต้มยำกุ้ง)

This shrimp soup is one of the most iconic dishes in Thai gastronomy. Fragrant with the aromas of lemongrass, Kaffir lime leaves and galangal, it is also tangy and very spicy. Although it is found all over the country, sometimes with seafood or fish, it is a staple of central Thai cuisine.

Yield: 4 servings
Prep time: 20 minutes
Cook time: 30 to 35 minutes

- 12 whole unshelled raw shrimp or prawns
- 3 stalks lemongrass
- 2 tomatoes
- 1 onion
- 6 oyster mushrooms
- 10 slices galangal
- 8 Kaffir lime leaves
- 4 cilantro roots (optional) + a few leaves
- 2 tsp. (10 ml) palm sugar
- 1 tsp. (5 ml) salt
- Neutral oil

SEASONING

- 2 tbsp. (30 ml) *nam prik pao* (Thai chili paste)
- 1 to 3 fresh chilies, thinly sliced
- Juice of 1½ limes
- 2 tbsp. (30 ml) fish sauce
- 2 tbsp. (30 ml) unsweetened evaporated milk (optional)

1 Shell the shrimp, saving the shells to make the stock: sweat the shells in a little oil, and then add 2½ cups (625 ml) water and a pinch of salt. Let simmer over low heat for 15 to 20 minutes. Strain the mixture to remove the shells and impurities, saving the liquid.

2 Cut the lemongrass in three and lightly crush the stems with the handle of your knife. Chop the tomatoes, onion and mushrooms, discarding any tough mushroom stems.

3 Heat the stock in a large pot. Add the lemongrass, galangal, Kaffir lime leaves, cilantro roots, salt and sugar. Let simmer for 5 minutes. Strain the mixture if necessary to remove any tough pieces.

4 Add the shrimp, tomatoes, onion and mushrooms. Cook for 2 minutes over high heat, and then add the seasonings.

5 Serve with a sprinkling of cilantro leaves.

MOO PALO (หมูพะโล้)

Moo palo, also called *khai palo*, is a very popular Chinese-Thai dish found all over the capital. It is particularly popular for children, since it is not at all spicy.

Yield: 6 servings
Prep time: 10 minutes
Cook time: 1½ hours

- 20 ounces (600 g) pork belly
- 10 ounces (300 g) firm tofu
- 8 hard-boiled eggs, peeled
- 2 ounces (60 g) palm sugar (or about ¼ cup/60 ml)
- 4 cloves garlic
- ½ tsp. (2 ml) black pepper
- 3 tbsp. (45 ml) light soy sauce
- 3 tbsp. (45 ml) dark soy sauce
- 1 tbsp. (15 ml) oyster sauce
- 2 tbsp. (30 ml) neutral cooking oil
- 2 tbsp. (30 ml) frying oil
- 1 tsp. (5 ml) salt
- Pickled garlic and mustard greens (optional)

SEASONING

- 4 whole cloves
- 2 cinnamon sticks
- 2 whole star anise
- 1 tsp. (5 ml) coriander seeds
- ½ tsp. (2 ml) Sichuan pepper
- 3 cilantro roots or 1 small bunch of cilantro stems

1. In a dry frying pan, toast the seasoning ingredients except for the cilantro roots. Place in a tea ball or wrap in a piece of cheesecloth and close tightly using the cilantro roots.
2. Chop the meat into bite-sized pieces. Mince the palm sugar and garlic.
3. Heat the cooking oil in a pot over high heat. Add the salt and brown the meat on all sides.
4. Lower the heat, add the palm sugar and let it melt and caramelize. Add enough water to fill the pot, and then add the garlic, pepper, sauces and prepared seasoning. Cover and let simmer for 1½ hours.
5. While the stock is simmering, press the tofu to remove excess water, and then pat it dry. Dice the tofu into bite-sized cubes and fry in a wok or pan until golden-brown around the edges. Remove the tofu from the pan and let it drain on paper towels.
6. Place the fried tofu and eggs in the pot at least 30 minutes before the end of the cooking time. After 1½ hours, the meat should be very tender.
7. Serve with white rice and pickled garlic and mustard greens.

SOUTHERN CUISINE

Southern Thailand's cuisine is strongly influenced by the region's coastal geography and trade with other countries. The southernmost provinces, which border Malaysia, formed the Pattani Kingdom until the early 20th century. It was a major trading port for Persian, Indian, Javanese, Portuguese, English and Dutch merchants and Malaysian and Chinese workers. Today, the south's gastronomy is as rich and diverse as its people.

It is a spicy cuisine that includes some of the country's hottest curries. The recipes are centered around seafood, the region's abundant coconut milk and local vegetables and herbs such as melinjo leaves (*bai liang*) and bitter beans (*sator*). Rhizomes such as turmeric and fingerroot are also widely used. The traditional green curry and *tom kha* soup of central Thailand take on a yellow hue with the addition of turmeric. Muslim Thais, who are numerous in the region, have their own delicacies, such as *khao mok*, a spicy variation on chicken and rice, and serve curries with pan-fried bread of Indian origin (similar to roti). Descendants of the Hokkiens, who came from southern China, prepare noodle dishes such as *mee hokkien*.

THE FLAVORS OF THE SOUTH

Southern Thailand's characteristic flavors are powerful and have a strong fishy aroma. Chilies and fish sauces such as *nam budu* are used generously. Salty and sour flavors are particularly popular, such as in the famous *gaeng som* fish curry and *gaeng tai pla*, a curry featuring a fish sauce made from fermented fish guts.

Bitter beans (*sator*; สะตอ): Also known as "stink beans" due to their strong flavor, these beans are grown in the south and widely consumed there.

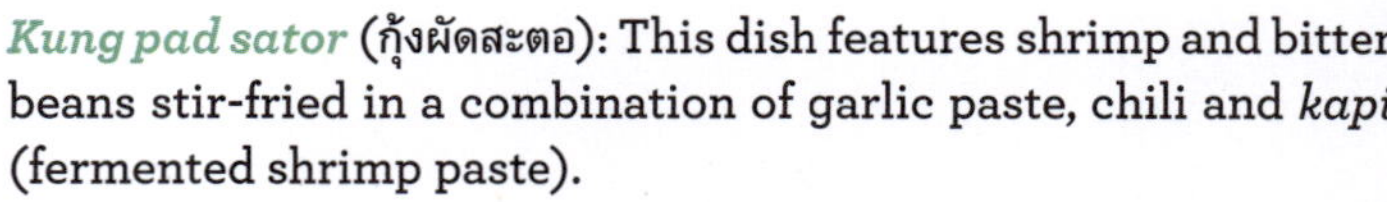

Kung pad sator (กุ้งผัดสะตอ): This dish features shrimp and bitter beans stir-fried in a combination of garlic paste, chili and *kapi* (fermented shrimp paste).

Gnetum (*bai liang*; ใบเหลียง): The leaves of this plant are used in a number of dishes that are staples in the daily lives of southern Thais. Gnetum leaves are also found in Indonesian cuisine.

Bai liang pad khai (ใบเหลียงผัดไข่): This dish is a stir-fry of eggs, gnetum leaves and garlic seasoned with *nam pla* fish sauce.

Tom kati pak liang (ต้มกะทิผักเหลียง): This dish is a coconut milk soup with gnetum leaves with or without shrimp and seasoned with *kapi* (fermented shrimp paste).

The island of Phuket, Thailand's largest, is now linked to the mainland by a road, and for centuries it was a center of international trade. The island's gastronomy is unique, born from a marriage of Chinese and Malay cultures. The descendants of those early settlers are called Peranakans. In 2015, Phuket became the first town in the whole of Asia to be designated a UNESCO Gastronomic City.

Pad mee hokkien

PHUKET SPECIALTIES

Noodles are a specialty of the Hokkien community, who eat them in a variety of ways: stir-fried, in soup, deep-fried ...

Pad mee hokkien (ผัดหมี่ฮกเกี้ยน): Thick egg noodles are stir-fried in a smoking-hot wok and seasoned with soy sauce and oyster sauce. They are served with Chinese broccoli, pork, sometimes shrimp, egg and a thick sauce.

Moo hong (หมูฮ้อง): Braised pork is sweetened with soy sauce and seasoned with black pepper, garlic, cilantro roots and star anise.

Mee hoon kraduk moo (หมี่หุ้นซุปกระดูกหมู): This dish of thin rice noodles stir-fried in soy sauce is served simply with garlic chives, fried shallots and a peppery broth made with pork bones.

Nam prik dips can be found all over the country, but Phuket has its own recipes, including the popular *nam chub yam* (น้ำชุบหยำ): shrimp paste and chilies are enhanced with boiled fish or shrimp and the acidity of lime.

Oh aeo (โอ้เอ๋ว): Phuket's signature dessert is *aiyu* jelly (made from the seeds of the fruit of the creeping fig) topped with finely crushed ice and syrup. It is often garnished with adzuki beans.

KHANOM JIN NAM YA (ขนมจีนน้ำยา)

This is a much-appreciated specialty of southern Thailand, particularly in Krabi and Trang. Rama II even mentioned this age-old curry in a famous 18th-century poem, and it remains one of Thailand's most popular curries.

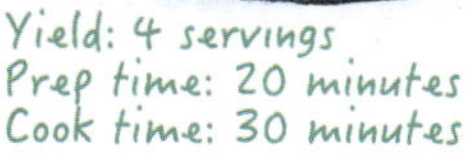

CURRY

- 14 ounces (400 g) fish fillet (such as cod)
- 13 ounces (375 g) rice vermicelli
- 15 dried chilies (or less)
- 10 slices galangal
- 4 sections fingerroot
- 2 stalks lemongrass
- ¾-inch (2 cm) piece fresh turmeric
- 3 cloves garlic
- 2 shallots
- 2 cups (500 ml) coconut milk
- 4 Kaffir lime leaves
- 1 tsp. (5 ml) shrimp paste
- 3 tbsp. (45 ml) fish sauce
- 1 tbsp. (15 ml) tamarind paste
- 1 tbsp. (15 ml) palm sugar

CHOICE OF ACCOMPANIMENTS

- 4 hard-boiled eggs, peeled and halved
- Stir-fried dried chilies
- 7 ounces (200 g) bean sprouts (about 1½ cups/375 ml)
- ¼ white cabbage, thinly sliced (about 1 cup/250 ml)
- Cucumber
- Long bean
- Pickled mustard greens
- Thai basil leaves
- Chinese cilantro leaves

1 Soak the dried chilies in lukewarm water. You can adjust the heat of the curry by removing some of the seeds.

2 Boil the rice vermicelli for 7 minutes, then rinse the noodles and shape them into small nests (you should have 3 to 4 nests per serving).

3 Make a stock with 1¼ cups (300 ml) water, 5 slices galangal, 1 stalk lemongrass that has been lightly crushed and 1 section of fingerroot chopped into a medium dice. Bring the mixture to a boil and poach the fish in it. Strain the stock, setting the liquid aside and flaking the fish (discard the aromatics and any fish bones).

4 Thinly slice the turmeric, remaining lemongrass, galangal and fingerroot. Mince the garlic and shallots. Using a mortar and pestle, crush the ingredients to form a paste.

5 In a saucepan, stir-fry the curry paste in a little coconut cream (the solids from the can of coconut milk), and then add the stock, fish, coconut milk and the rest of the curry ingredients.

6 Arrange the eggs, fried chilies and vegetables on a plate, and place at the center of the table. Place 3 or 4 nests of rice vermicelli in each bowl, cover generously with curry and serve.

KAENG SOM (แกงส้มใต้)

Kaeng som means "sour curry," and it is one of southern Thailand's spiciest and most beloved dishes. For many, it is a daily treat. Reminiscent of a fish soup, this curry is tangy from the tamarind and intensified by the curry paste made with chilies and turmeric.

Yield: 4 servings
Prep time: 30 minutes
Cook time: 10 minutes

CURRY PASTE

- 15 dried long chilies
- 15 fresh green or red Thai chilies
- 1 tsp. (5 ml) salt
- 2-inch (5 cm) piece turmeric
- 5 cloves garlic
- 2 shallots
- 1 tsp. (5 ml) shrimp paste

OTHER INGREDIENTS

- 1 whole fish (such as sea bass or sea bream), gutted and cut into steaks
- 7 ounces (200 g) green papaya (about 1 small)
- 3 tbsp. (45 ml) tamarind pulp
- 3 tbsp. (45 ml) fish sauce
- 1½ tsp. (7 ml) palm sugar
- 1 tbsp. (15 ml) lime juice

1. Prepare the curry paste with a mortar and pestle, starting by crushing the chilies and salt together, then adding the rest of the ingredients in the order listed.
2. Thinly slice the papaya.
3. Bring 2¾ cups (675 ml) water to a gentle boil in a saucepan and then stir in the curry paste. Add the papaya, tamarind pulp, fish sauce and palm sugar. Cook for 5 minutes.
4. Add the fish and cook for 3 to 5 minutes.
5. Remove from the heat, add the lime juice and serve with jasmine rice.

OTHER SPECIALTIES

Khao yam (ข้าวยำ) is a southern Thai rice salad. The rice is served with a wide variety of fresh aromatic herbs, tangy fruits, thinly sliced raw vegetables, chilies, toasted coconut meat and chopped dried shrimp. The whole dish is enhanced with *nam budu* sauce and lime. This dish is usually eaten for breakfast.

Khua kling (คั่วกลิ้ง) is a simple and very popular dry ground meat curry. A curry paste is prepared before being lightly browned, usually with pork or beef.

POPULAR DISHES

Thai cuisine is considered among the best in the world. And yet, the most popular dishes inside the country have rarely crossed its borders and remain mostly unknown in the rest of the world. While *pad thai* is the national dish in the eyes of visitors, *pad kaprao* (ผัดกะเพรา), a basil stir-fry whose volume of chilies sets the palate ablaze, undoubtedly takes first place in Thais' hearts. Thais enjoy noodles in all their forms, but they most often eat them in a bowl of soup. In this chapter, you will also discover *nam prik* (น้ำพริก), which is a very old and traditional dish still eaten daily in every corner of the country. Finally, you will discover the great wealth of curries, which can be served in form of a broth or a creamy sauce or stir-fried in a wok. Whatever their form, curries are invariably accompanied by noodles, rice or even pan-fried bread.

THE NATIONAL DISH: *PAD KAPRAO* (ผัดกะเพรา)

A simple, quick and comforting dish, *pad kaprao* is undoubtedly the Thai favorite for lunch on the run. It means "stir-fry with holy basil."

Pad kaprao is available with a variety of proteins: ground pork (the most popular), crispy pork, chicken, beef, century eggs, shrimp or other seafood. It is so popular that the country's tourism authority organized a national competition for the best recipe, the World Kraprao Thailand Grand Prix!

It is prepared by stir-frying lots of minced garlic and chilies in a smoking-hot wok before adding the chosen protein, soy sauce, oyster sauce, fish sauce, a little sugar and, last but not least, the essential holy basil (*bai kaprao*; ใบกะเพรา). It is served with a fried egg and jasmine rice.

PAD KAPRAO MOU SAP (ผัดกะเพราหมูสับ):

Ground pork stir-fried with holy basil

Fried egg

Holy basil

Jasmine rice

Ground pork

PAD KAPRAO KAI KHAI DAO
ผัดกะเพราไก่ไข่ดาว

Yield: 4 servings
Prep time: 15 minutes
Cook time: 15 minutes

- 21 ounces (600 g) chicken breast
- 3 to 4 ounces (100 g) long beans (optional)
- 1 onion
- 4 to 10 bird's eye chilies
- 8 cloves garlic
- 2 tbsp. (30 ml) oyster sauce
- 2 tbsp. (30 ml) light soy sauce
- 2 tbsp. (30 ml) dark soy sauce
- 2 tbsp. (30 ml) fish sauce
- 2 tsp. (10 ml) confectioners' sugar
- 1 cup (250 ml) frying oil
- 4 eggs
- 2 bunches holy basil
- ¼ cup (60 ml) neutral vegetable oil
- 1 tsp. (5 ml) ground white pepper

1 Finely chop the chicken. Thinly slice the beans. Mince the onion. Remove the seeds from some of the chilies to control the heat. Crush the chilies and garlic together with a mortar and pestle.

2 Stir together the sauces, sugar and ¼ cup (60 ml) water in a bowl.

3 Heat the frying oil in a pan and fry the eggs one at time. The whites should be bubbly with crispy, brown edges. Transfer the cooked eggs to paper towels. This is the Thai version of a sunny side up egg (*khai dao*).

4 Fry a handful of basil leaves to crisp them up, and then place them on paper towel.

5 Heat the neutral vegetable oil in a wok over medium heat and brown the garlic-chili mixture. Add the chicken and sear over high heat until it is cooked through.

6 Add the sauce-sugar mixture, beans and onion to the wok and stir-fry over high heat for 1 minute.

7 Turn off the heat, and then add the white pepper and fresh basil. Stir for a few seconds.

8 Serve the chicken with jasmine rice and top with fried basil leaves, a fried egg and *prik nam pla*.

NAM PRIK (น้ำพริก)

WHAT IS IT?

Nam prik (น้ำพริก) is undoubtedly the oldest dish in the Kingdom of Thailand. Little known outside the country, it is nevertheless part of the local population's staple diet. It was originally used to season rice and served with a protein that was fermented to preserve it, such as shrimp paste. Its name gives some clues about its consistency and flavor profile: *nam* means "water" and *prik* means "chili." However, it is not always as spicy as its name suggests. Today, there are over a hundred variations with assorted textures. *Nam prik* is prepared with a mortar and pestle: raw, cooked, grilled, fried or fermented foods are blended to produce a spicy puree, which is served with rice and a selection of raw or boiled vegetables for dipping.

THE BASIC INGREDIENTS

Nam prik was originally a simple recipe made with *kapi* (fermented shrimp paste), garlic, shallots and chilies. The addition of ingredients and seasonings such as sugar, lime, tamarind, herbs, fruit, meats and fish created numerous variations.

POPULAR NAM PRIK

Nam prik kapi (น้ำพริกกะปิ) is one of the country's oldest and most popular versions. It is primarily associated with the central region of Thailand and is prepared with *kapi* that has been grilled to release its aromas. Chilies, garlic, shallots and pea eggplants are added to the mix. The dip is seasoned with lime, a little palm sugar and fish sauce. *Nam prik kapi* is often served with fried mackerel (*pla tu*) and raw vegetables. It serves as a base for other *nam prik* recipes.

Nam prik kung siap (น้ำพริกกุ้งเสียบ) is one of the most popular versions of *nam prik* in southern Thailand. It is made with garlic, shallots, chilies, *kapi* and small dried shrimp that have been fried, which gives the dish a bit of crunch. It is seasoned with palm sugar, lime and fish sauce. It is served with herbs and raw vegetables.

NAM PRIK ONG (น้ำพริกอ่อง)

Originally from northern Thailand, *nam prik ong* is one of the few *nam prik* that is only mildly spicy. It is served with sticky rice, assorted vegetables and pork crackers.

Yield: 4 servings
Prep time: 35 minutes
Cook time: 15 minutes
Soak time: 10 minutes

CHILI PASTE

- 5 dried long red chilies
- ½ tsp. (2 ml) salt
- 1 stalk lemongrass, bottom 4 inches (10 cm) only, thinly sliced
- 2 shallots
- 4 cloves garlic
- 1 patty roasted *tua nao* (optional) or 1 tsp. (5 ml) shrimp paste
- 15 red or yellow cherry tomatoes

OTHER INGREDIENTS

- 3 tbsp. (45 ml) lard or neutral vegetable oil
- 5 ounces (150 g) ground pork loin
- 2 tbsp. (30 ml) fish sauce
- ½ tsp. (2 ml) palm sugar or brown sugar
- Thinly sliced cilantro

1 Soak the dried chilies for 10 minutes in warm water to rehydrate them.

2 Prepare the chili paste using a mortar and pestle. Start with the rehydrated chili peppers and salt, and then add the remaining ingredients one at a time in the order listed.

3 Heat the lard in a wok and stir-fry the chili paste for 2 minutes to release its aromas.

4 Add the pork, fish sauce and sugar, and stir-fry until the meat is cooked through.

5 Serve with sticky rice and the raw vegetables of your choice, and top with thinly sliced cilantro leaves.

Nam prik long rua (น้ำพริกลงเรือ) was created in the royal kitchens and is undoubtedly one of the most complex dishes to prepare, as it requires various methods and steps. Its name refers to how it came about: One of King Rama V's wives had to hastily prepare a picnic for a boat trip (*rua*), and all she had to work with was leftovers. The preparation was a sweet-and-sour *nam prik* that was an immediate success.

The dish consists of a base of *nam prik kapi* to which sweet pork (*moo wan*) and fried flaked catfish (*pla duk fu*) are added. It is served with rice, salted duck eggs, marinated garlic, raw vegetables and aromatic herbs.

NOODLE SOUPS
ก๋วยเตี๋ยว

Thais eat a bowl of noodle soup on the go nearly every day, at any time of the day or night!

You will find these soups in cafeterias, food courts, restaurants and especially at the numerous food stalls that line streets all over the country. *Kouay tiew* refers more specifically to rice noodles, but it is also commonly used to refer to any noodle soup. There is a wide variety: white, egg or rice noodles, meats and different seasonings. You can order a bowl of noodle soup with or without broth. In the latter case, they are known as "dry noodles" (*heng*; แห้ง). You can even order a bowl of noodle soup with a protein, vegetables and broth — but without noodles!

THE MOST POPULAR SOUPS

Kouay tiew nam sai (ก๋วยเตี๋ยวน้ำใส): This noodle soup's clear broth is made with pork, chicken or beef and is seasoned with cilantro, pepper and fried garlic. It is served with a choice of meats. The simple, salty broth also serves as a base for other soups.

Kouay tiew rua (ก๋วยเตี๋ยวเรือ): This dish has a long history and a hint of nostalgia. It takes its name from the boats on which it was sold when Bangkok's main waterways were still in use. In homage to that period, *kouay tiew rua* is sometimes served in a boat-shaped bowl. Its unique broth contains pig's blood, giving it a rich texture, taste and color.

Kouay tiew tom yam (ก๋วยเตี๋ยวต้มยำ): This is one of Thailand's favorite soups, with a clear broth seasoned with a *nam prik pao* chili puree, lime, sugar, fish sauce and dried chilies. It also contains crushed peanuts and various cubed or ground meats or fish balls.

Ba mi heng (บะหมี่แห้ง): *Ba mi* refers to egg noodles and *heng* to the fact that they are served dry, with the broth on the side. These noodles, of Chinese origin, are usually served with barbecue pork (*moo dang*) or crispy pork (*moo krob*), blanched cabbage (*pak kwang tung*) and boiled or fried wontons.

Yen ta fo (เย็นตาโฟ): This soup is instantly recognizable by its bright pink broth. Its color comes from cubes of fermented soy. It is usually served with rice noodles, fish or shrimp dumplings, tofu and calamari or meat; cubes of coagulated pig's blood called *luad moo* (เลือดหมู), blanched water spinach and fried wontons are sometimes added.

The noodles are served as soon as they are ready together with the broth. If you would like your noodles without broth, specify *kor kuay tiaw heng ka/krap* (ขอก๋วยเตี๋ยวแห้ง ค่ะ/ครับ).

RICE NOODLES

Broad noodles

Kouay tiew sen yai (เส้นใหญ่)

Medium noodles

Kouay tiew sen lek (เส้นเล็ก)

Thin noodles

Kouay tiew sen mi (เส้นหมี่)

WHEAT NOODLES

Sen ba mi (เส้นบะหมี่)

RICE NOODLE ROLLS

Kouay jap (กวยจั๊บ)

SOYBEAN VERMICELLI

Woon sen (วุ้นเส้น)

Beef

Nua (เนื้อ)

Duck

Ped (เป็ด)

Pork

Moo (หมู)

Barbecue pork

Moo dang (หมูแดง)

Crispy pork

Moo krob (หมูกรอบ)

Pork blood

Luad moo (เลือดหมู)

Offal

Krueng nai (เครื่องใน)

Beef balls

Luk chin nua (ลูกชิ้นเนื้อ)

Pork balls

Luk chin moo (ลูกชิ้นหมู)

Fish balls

Luk chin pla (ลูกชิ้นปลา)

Shrimp

Kung (กุ้ง)

Calamari

Plamuk (ปลาหมึก)

Tofu

Taohu (เต้าหู้)

CURRIES (แกง)

Curries are almost certainly the quintessential element of the Thai culinary identity, with specialties differing from region to region and even from city to city.

A multitude of dishes based on *prik kaeng* (แกง) curry paste are categorized under the name *kaeng* (พริกแกง), which translates to curry. Curry paste can require few or many ingredients, which are usually ground together with a granite mortar and pestle. These ingredients range from chilies to aromatic herbs to spices, not to mention the fermented foods that provide salt and umami. Once the paste is made, it is used to give curries their distinctive aroma. The curry itself can take the form of a boiled soup, a creamy sauce made with coconut milk or a stir-fried meat dish. In every case, the dish is complemented with various vegetables, meats or fish.

There are everyday curries, commonly found in food courts and at *raan khao kaeng* (ร้านข้าวแกง), the stalls offering a wide variety of dishes with a plate of rice that you can garnish with the toppings of your choice. There are also curries for festivals and celebrations that require several days to prepare and skilled helpers, royal curries concocted with highly prized ingredients, and the more rustic country or jungle curries called *kaeng pa* (แกงป่า).

Coconut milk curry
Kaeng paneng
แกงพะแนง

Clear curry
Kaeng om
แกงอ่อม

Dry curry
Khua kling
คั่วกลิ้ง

PREPARING A CURRY PASTE

1 Toast the spices and dried chilies in a dry pan. Roast or stir-fry the garlic, shallots, shrimp paste or *tua nao* soybean cake.

2 Grind each spice separately with a granite mortar and pestle.

3 Chop all of the aromatics (lemongrass, galangal, turmeric, fingerroot, etc.).

4 Crush all the ingredients with a mortar and pestle, starting with the fresh or dried chilies and the salt, which will help break down the rest of the ingredients. Add the ingredients from hardest and driest to softest and wettest, creating a smooth paste. Be sure to puree each ingredient before adding the next.

GREEN CURRY CHICKEN (แกงเขียวหวานไก่)

The green curry chicken (*kaeng kiew wan kai*; แกงเขียวหวานไก่) associated with Thailand's central region is one of the country's most popular dishes. It is served in nearly every cafeteria, food court and restaurant in the country.

Yield: 4 servings
Prep time: 1 hour
Cook time: 25 to 30 minutes

GREEN CURRY PASTE

- 8 to 10 green Thai chilies
- 2 *prik chi fa* or other long green chilies
- 2 tsp. (10 ml) salt
- Zest from ½ Kaffir lime
- 2 tsp. (10 ml) coriander seeds, toasted
- 2 tsp. (10 ml) cumin seeds, toasted
- ½ tsp. (2 ml) ground white pepper
- 3 stalks lemongrass, top 4 inches (10 cm) only, chopped
- 1-inch (3 cm) piece galangal, chopped
- 2 cilantro roots or 2 tsp. (10 ml) minced cilantro stems
- 6 cloves garlic
- 2 large shallots, chopped
- 1 tsp. (5 ml) shrimp paste

OTHER INGREDIENTS

- 21 ounces (600 g) boneless chicken thighs
- 8 round green Thai eggplants
- 1 handful pea eggplants
- 1 long red chili
- 1 tbsp. (15 ml) vegetable oil
- 3¼ cups (800 ml) coconut milk
- 8 to 10 Kaffir lime leaves
- 2½ tbsp. (37 ml) palm sugar or brown sugar
- 3 to 4 tbsp. (45–60 ml) fish sauce
- 1 bunch sweet Thai basil

1. Prepare the curry paste with a mortar and pestle, blending the ingredients in the order listed.
2. Chop the chicken into bite-size pieces. Quarter the round eggplants. Thinly slice the long red chili.
3. Stir-fry 4 tbsp. (60 ml) curry paste with vegetable oil and 3 tbsp. (45 ml) coconut cream (the solids from a can of coconut milk) for a few minutes. When the oil rises to the surface and separates from the paste, add the chicken. Stir-fry for a few minutes.
4. Add the remaining coconut milk, Kaffir lime leaves, palm sugar, fish sauce and eggplants. Cook for 12 to 15 minutes, until the eggplants are cooked through.
5. Finish the curry by adding the sliced chili and the basil leaves.
6. Adjust the seasoning if desired and serve with white rice or *khanom jin* rice vermicelli.

RED CURRY DUCK (แกงเผ็ดเป็ดย่าง)

Red curry (*kaeng pet*; แกงเผ็ด) is a very popular dish. There are many variations with meats and vegetables. This curry paste is also used to make fish fritters (*thod man pla*; ทอดมันปลา) and a steamed fish custard (*hor mok*; ห่อหมก).

Yield: 4 servings
Prep time: 1 hour
Cook time: 25 to 30 minutes

RED CURRY PASTE

- 12 dried red chilies, rehydrated, deseeded and drained
- 2 tsp. (10 ml) salt
- Zest from ½ Kaffir lime
- 1 tsp. (5 ml) coriander seeds, toasted
- ½ tsp. (2 ml) cumin seeds, toasted
- 1 tsp. (5 ml) ground white pepper
- 3 stalks lemongrass, top 4 inches (10 cm) only, chopped
- 1-inch (3 cm) piece galangal, chopped
- 2 cilantro roots or 2 tbsp. (30 ml) minced cilantro stems
- 6 cloves garlic
- 4 shallots, chopped
- 1 tsp. (5 ml) shrimp paste

OTHER INGREDIENTS

- 21-ounce (600 g) whole duck or 2 duck breasts
- 3¼ cups (800 ml) coconut milk
- 3 tbsp. (45 ml) palm sugar
- 8 Kaffir lime leaves
- 12 cherry tomatoes
- ⅔ cup (250 ml) diced pineapple (drained if using canned)
- 3 to 6 tbsp. (45–90 ml) fish sauce
- ½ bunch sweet Thai basil, leaves only

1. Prepare the curry paste with a mortar and pestle, blending the ingredients in the order listed.
2. Score the duck skin with a knife, and then cook it skin-side down in a pan over medium heat for 15 minutes. Skim off the rendered fat as you go, reserving 2 tbsp. (30 ml) of it. Turn the meat over and cook for a further 3 minutes. Leave to rest for 15 minutes, and then thinly slice it.
3. In a large saucepan or Dutch oven, stir-fry 3 tbsp. (45 ml) curry paste in the reserved duck fat and 3 tbsp. (45 ml) coconut cream (the solids from a can of coconut milk) for a few minutes.
4. When the oil comes to the surface and separates from the paste, add the palm sugar, remaining coconut milk, Kaffir lime leaves, cherry tomatoes and pineapple. Let simmer 3 minutes.
5. Gradually add the fish sauce.
6. Adjust the seasoning if desired. Serve the curry with jasmine rice and topped with basil leaves.

MASSAMAN CURRY CHICKEN
แกงมัสมั่นไก่

Massaman curry has been a popular dish for centuries and was originally reserved for celebrations. King Rama II even alluded to it in a poem extolling the virtues of his wife Phra Sri Suriyendramataya, whose culinary talents remain legendary. This dish is very popular with the Thai Muslim community, who created it. It is also cooked with beef or, more rarely, mutton and served with pan-fried bread.

Yield: 4 servings
Prep time: 1½ hours
Cook time: 1 hour

MASSAMAN CURRY PASTE

- 12 dried long peppers, deseeded and roasted
- 1 tsp. (5 ml) salt
- 3 cilantro roots or 3 tbsp. (45 ml) minced cilantro stems
- 3 stalks lemongrass, top 4 inches (10 cm) only, chopped
- 9 cloves garlic
- 3 shallots, chopped
- 1 tsp. (5 ml) shrimp paste

DRY SPICES, TO BE TOASTED AND GROUND

- 2 blades mace
- 1 cinnamon stick
- 2 tsp. (10 ml) coriander seeds
- 2 tsp. (10 ml) cumin seeds
- 3 cardamom pods, seeds only
- ½ nutmeg seed
- 2 tsp. (10 ml) white pepper

OTHER INGREDIENTS

- 2 chicken quarters
- 8 medium potatoes
- Oil for frying
- 1 tsp. (5 ml) turmeric (optional)
- 3¼ cups (800 ml) coconut milk
- 2 handfuls unsalted roasted peanuts
- 1 handful golden raisins
- 4 bay leaves
- 2 tbsp. (30 ml) fish sauce
- 2 tbsp. (30 ml) tamarind juice
- 2 tbsp. (30 ml) palm sugar
- 6 small shallots
- Juice from ½ bitter orange, such as Seville (optional)
- Neutral vegetable oil for cooking

1. Prepare the curry paste with a mortar and pestle, blending the ingredients in the order listed.
2. Separate the chicken drumsticks from the thighs, and chop the thighs in two through the bone. Peel and dice the potatoes.
3. Heat a little oil in a pan on high heat and brown the potatoes.
4. In another pan, brown the chicken skin-side down in hot oil, adding turmeric if desired (this will color the chicken a nice shade of yellow).
5. In a deep saucepan or Dutch oven, heat 2 tbsp. (30 ml) oil over medium heat. Stir-fry 2 tbsp. (30 ml) curry paste diluted with 2 tbsp. (30 ml) coconut cream (the solids from a can of coconut milk). Stir until the moisture evaporates and the oil separates.
6. Add the remaining coconut milk, potatoes, chicken, peanuts, raisins, bay leaves, fish sauce, tamarind juice and sugar to the curry. Simmer for at least 1 hour.
7. Add the whole shallots and cook for 10 minutes, just until they soften.
8. Take the pot off the heat, add the orange juice if using and serve with jasmine rice or pan-fried bread.

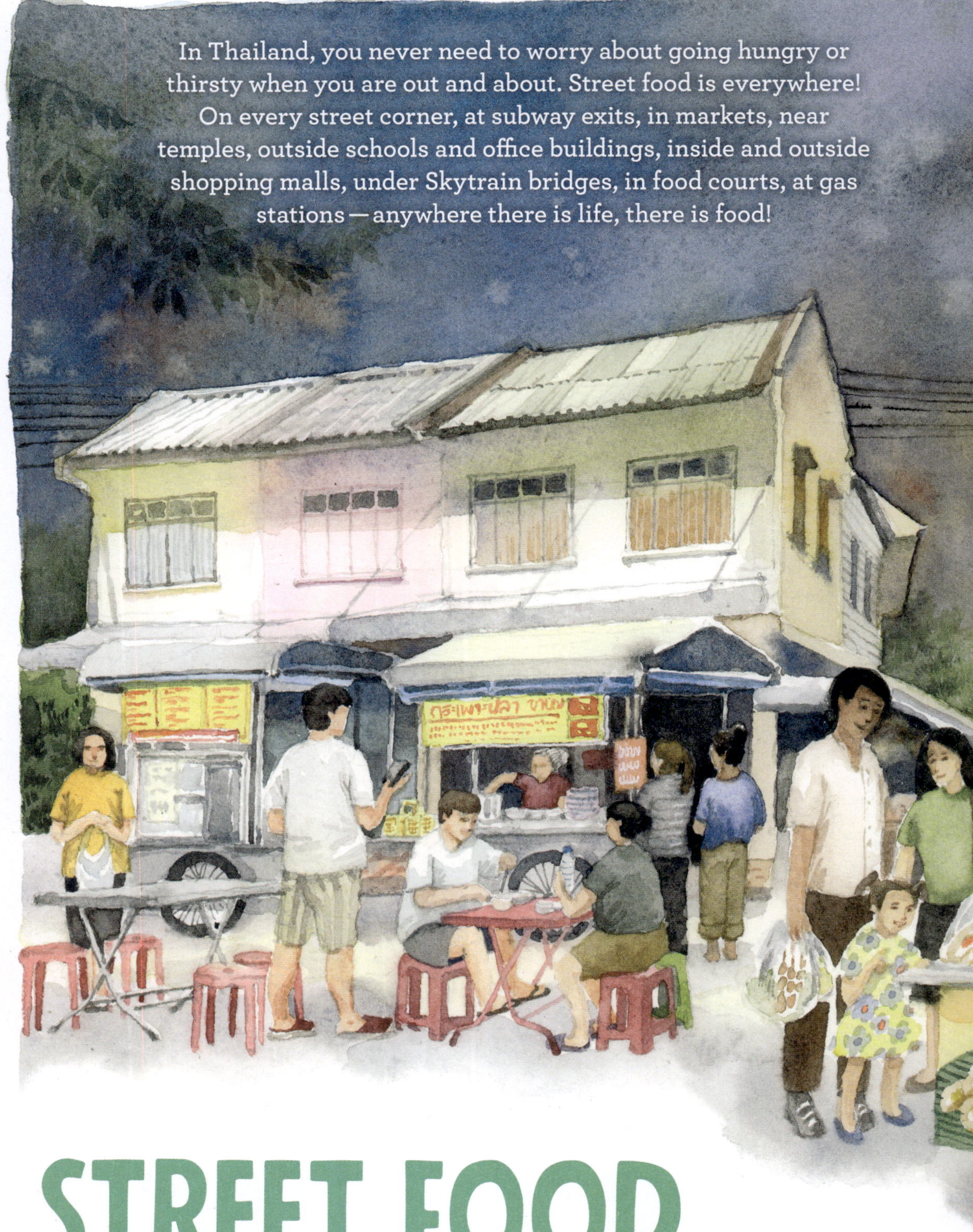

In Thailand, you never need to worry about going hungry or thirsty when you are out and about. Street food is everywhere! On every street corner, at subway exits, in markets, near temples, outside schools and office buildings, inside and outside shopping malls, under Skytrain bridges, in food courts, at gas stations — anywhere there is life, there is food!

STREET FOOD

You can find street food vendors day or night, particularly in the capital. Bangkok actually has a nickname that combines two other famous city nicknames: "the city of angels that never sleeps." Every stall has their specialty. Some of these dishes are so fresh and masterfully prepared that even the famous Red Guide has begun to recognize talented street cooks.

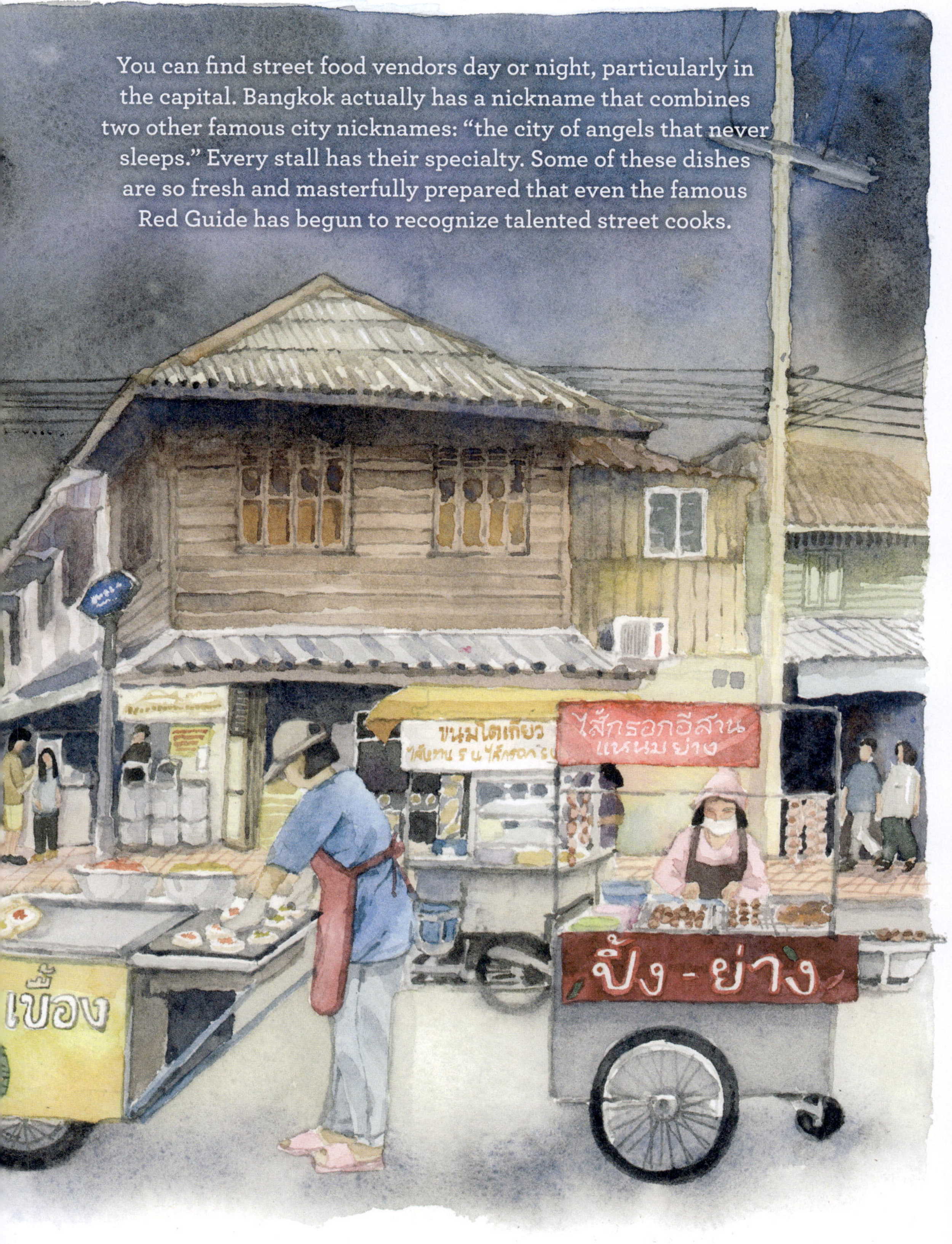

BANGKOK'S STREET FOOD

เยาวราช

YAOWARAT CHINATOWN BANGKOK

Bangkok is a veritable open-air restaurant! In a country where there is not much in the way of a social safety net, construction and street food are often the only way for immigrants and those in reduced circumstances to earn a living. In this megalopolis of 11 million people, eating out is often easier, cheaper and healthier than shopping and cooking for yourself. You can usually enjoy a delicious meal for less than a dollar. Discover some of the neighborhoods with unmissable street food.

THE EAST BANK OF CHINATOWN

At dusk, around six in the evening, the streets along Yaowarat Avenue come alive. Street vendors and stallholders set up their carts and tables, and the streets quickly fill up with locals and tourists alike. The specialties offered in this neighborhood are, understandably, mainly Chinese. The area is renowned for its street food, and you will often have to wait in line to get served!

SOME OF THE NEIGHBORHOOD'S SPECIALTIES

Egg noodles (*ba mi*; บะหมี่) served with pork or Peking duck are a must and found on nearly every street corner.

Fried oyster or mussel omelet (*hoi thod*; หอยทอด) is a specialty that resulted from the marriage of Chinese and Thai cuisines.

Chao kouay (เฉาก๊วย) is a refreshing beverage with seaweed jelly and sugar syrup. It is served hot or over ice.

Bird's nest soup (*rang nok*; รังนก) is a rare and sought-after delicacy. It is made from the mucus that particular birds use to build their nests. Renowned for its therapeutic properties, this dish is served hot or cold.

WEST BANK OF TALAT PHLU

Talat Phlu, named after the old betel leaf market that historically took place there, is located on the west bank of the Chao Praya River, in the Thonburi District. Betel has now given way to a street food scene that is buzzing from morning to night under the bridge, in the surrounding streets and along the tracks at Talat Phlu Station. The relaxed atmosphere of this historic Chinese area is the opposite of today's Chinatown.

ARI: A TRENDY NEIGHBORHOOD

Located in northern Bangkok, at the foot of the Ari Skytrain Station (or Ari BTS), this neighborhood is home to both "cutting-edge" restaurants and a wide variety of street stalls. There is something for everyone! This contrast is typical of Bangkok, where street vendors can be found among skyscrapers and luxury shopping malls, combining tradition and modernity.

PAD THAI

In the eyes of the world, *pad thai* is Thailand's national dish. And yet, it only very recently arrived on the culinary scene. It was first concocted by the chef of Prime Minister Plaek Phibunsongkhram, who loved it and whose influence elevated it to the status of national dish!

THE HISTORY

In the 1930s, Thailand was caught between British Burma and French Indochina. To fend off European colonial ambitions, Prime Minister Phibun sought to unite the population, fostering a sense of national unity across the then very diverse territory of Siam. He launched a national policy to modernize the country. The Kingdom of Siam was renamed Thailand, literally the land of the Thai people, and various reforms were undertaken: a new national anthem, a unified language, the use of forks and spoons at the table and the promotion of Thai stir-fried noodles (*kouay tiew pad thai*) as the national dish.

The prime minister also encouraged the export of rice (to the detriment of local consumption) to boost the country's economy and launched a massive campaign with the slogan "noodles for lunch!" Noodles, which were mainly cooked by the Chinese immigrant population, started to become more popular. The *pad thai* recipe was widely distributed throughout the country. The government even provided free carts for street vendors to set up shop and sell *pad thai*! The famous noodle dish, stir-fried with tamarind, has since become Thailand's culinary trademark throughout the world.

Yield: 2 servings
Prep time: 5 minutes
Cook time: 10 minutes

- 9 ounces (250 g) fresh flat rice noodles (*sen lek*) or 4 to 5 ounces (125 g) dry noodles, soaked in cold water for at least 1 hour
- 8 raw shrimp
- ¼ cup (60 ml) tamarind pulp
- ¼ cup (60 ml) fish sauce
- 2 tbsp. (30 ml) palm sugar, finely chopped
- 5 cloves garlic
- 4 sprigs garlic chives or scallions
- 2 ounces (50 g) firm tofu (optional)
- Neutral vegetable oil
- 2 tbsp. (30 ml) minced pickled radish (optional)
- 2 large handfuls bean sprouts
- 2 eggs
- ¼ cup (60 ml) unsalted roasted peanuts
- 2 lime wedges
- 2 tsp. (10 ml) chili flakes

1. In a bowl, stir together the tamarind pulp, fish sauce, 3 tbsp. (45 ml) water and chopped sugar until the sugar dissolves.
2. Shell and devein the shrimp, cutting along the entire length of the back to remove the intestine.
3. Mince the garlic, roughly chop the chives or scallions and dice the tofu. Beat the eggs in a separate bowl.
4. Heat 2 tbsp. (30 ml) oil in a wok over high heat and lightly fry the shrimp for 1 minute on each side. Set aside.
5. In the same wok, heat 3 tbsp. (45 ml) oil over medium heat. Stir-fry the garlic until it begins to brown. Add the radishes, tofu, noodles and sauce to the wok, and stir-fry over high heat until the sauce is almost absorbed. Add the bean sprouts and stir-fry for a further 1 minute.
6. Place the noodle mixture on one side of the wok, add the eggs to the other and scramble them.
7. Add the chives or scallions and shrimp and stir-fry for 1 minute.
8. Just before serving, top the noodles with crushed peanuts. Garnish with a lime wedge and chili flakes.

FOOD COURTS

Large food courts can comprise a multitude of food and drink counters. Just like in North America, food courts can be found in nearly every shopping mall. They also offer a wide choice of dishes in one place and do not cost much more than the food at street stalls. They are very popular with Thais, who prefer to escape the heat outside and eat in air-conditioned spaces.

You can sometimes buy a prepaid card credited with the amount of your choice and use it to pay at any food counter

Some food courts offer a real change of scenery, both in terms of the visuals and the flavors, such as the Icon Siam mall, where the decor takes you through a magnificent historic floating market.

Food Court

MOO PING (หมูปิ้ง)

Skewers of grilled marinated pork are a street food staple. Sold for 10 baht (about 30 cents) each, they are eaten at any time of day, with or without sticky rice, as a quick snack on the go.

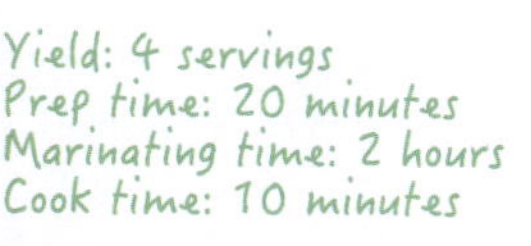

Yield: 4 servings
Prep time: 20 minutes
Marinating time: 2 hours
Cook time: 10 minutes

- 18 ounces (500 g) pork loin or other fatty cut of pork
- 5 cloves garlic
- 4 cilantro roots or 2 tbsp. (30 ml) minced cilantro stems
- 3 tbsp. (45 ml) palm sugar or brown sugar
- 1 cup (250 ml) coconut cream
- 2 tbsp. (30 ml) oyster sauce
- 2 tbsp. (30 ml) dark soy sauce
- 2 tbsp. (30 ml) light soy sauce
- 2 tbsp. (30 ml) neutral vegetable oil
- 1 tsp. (5 ml) ground white pepper

1. Chop the pork into bite-sized pieces, conserving the fat to keep it tender and flavorful as it cooks.
2. Prepare the marinade: Crush the garlic, cilantro roots and sugar with a mortar and pestle, and then mix in the rest of the ingredients.
3. Add the marinade to the meat, combine well and let sit for at least 2 hours in a cool place. You can also prepare the pork and marinade the day before and leave the pork to marinate overnight. While the pork is marinating, soak bamboo skewers in water to prevent them from burning as the meat cooks.
4. Prepare the skewers, and then barbecue them for a few minutes on each side.
5. Serve with sticky rice and green papaya salad for a complete meal.

Tip: If you do not have a barbecue, you can place the skewers under the broiler at 400°F (200°C) for 10 to 15 minutes. Turn the skewers halfway through, so they cook evenly on both sides.

Sanouk (สนุก) — which can mean fun, a joke, an amused look or a smile — is an integral part of Thai culture. It is a core value that we try to cultivate in every context and from the earliest age. For example, play is at the heart of pedagogy in schools. *Sanouk* is also the antidote to seriousness and can help alleviate life's difficulties.

During funeral ceremonies, which can last three to seven days, prayers, visits and music alternate day and night to accompany the deceased and his or her family.

IMPORTANT CELEBRATIONS

In a country where Buddhist religious celebrations, royal birthdays and local festivals come one after the other, there are many occasions to celebrate, and these celebrations set the rhythm of people's daily lives. The New Year is celebrated on three occasions: firstly, the Western New Year on January 1, then the Chinese New Year based on the lunar calendar in early February and, finally, the Thai Buddhist New Year, called *songkran* (สงกรานต์) in April. There is plenty of opportunity for the fun so dear to Thais!

WEDDINGS

In Thailand, marriage follows a ritual with very precise steps.

THE DAY'S SEQUENCE OF EVENTS

The morning begins with an early religious ceremony: Nine monks are invited to recite prayers and bless the bride and groom. Offerings of food are presented to the monks. After the meal, the monks leave. Usually at 9:09 in the morning (discover the symbolism of the number 9 on p. 106), the *khan mak* procession (ขันหมาก), led by the groom and his family, begins. They carry a *khan mak,* which is a floral arrangement featuring leaves with gifts that symbolize good luck that is placed on a golden tray or bowl. The procession is joyously accompanied by dancers and drums.

The groom then makes his way to the bride's room, passing through symbolic gates of garlands of flowers or golden chains held by the bridesmaids. Each time he passes through a "gate," he is required to pay an ever-increasing tribute to the gatekeeper. It is the most fun time of the ceremony, and all manner of jokes and merrymaking are encouraged.

When the bride and groom are reunited, a dowry, called a *sinsod* (สินสอด), is presented by the groom's parents to the bride's parents. It is then counted. It can contain money, jewelry and even property deeds. This an ancient tradition that continues only symbolically today. The dowry is not required, and if it is offered, it goes to the couple as a wedding gift and is often used to pay for the ceremony. The couple then exchange rings in front of their parents, and the groom can present the bride with other jewelry as well.

Next, the most important moment of the ceremony takes place, the one that seals the union: A *mongkhon* (มงคล), a crown of interlaced threads blessed by monks, is placed on the heads of the bride and groom. Starting with the oldest, guests take turns pouring holy water from a conch shell onto the couple's hands. The bride and groom then pay their respects to the elders and receive their blessings in return. To complete the ritual, the couple are taken back to their room, where the bed is adorned with objects designed to bring them luck throughout their union.

Once the morning ceremony is over, everyone returns home to rest and change into regular clothes before gathering for the wedding meal. Depending on the region, some aspects of the ceremony may vary, such as the dishes served during the meal. However, fermented rice vermicelli (*khanom jin*; ขนมจีน) is a staple of wedding menus: the noodles' length symbolizes the longevity of the union. Vermicelli is cooked all over the country and served with different regional curries. While the noodles are usually white, they are often dyed beautiful colors for the occasion.

Khanom jin for a wedding

THE NINE WEDDING DESSERTS

WHY NINE?

Astrology and numerology play important roles in Thais' daily life. This is a country where ghosts and *phi* (ผี) spirits rub shoulders with the living. No action is random or left to chance. Thais avoid making hasty, ill-considered choices, which may provoke spirits or deities and attract bad luck. Whether it is the date of a wedding or other important event, a license plate or a telephone number, Thais choose symbolic numbers.

Astrologers can easily be found on street corners.

The lucky numbers are three, which brings harmony and balance; seven, which symbolizes luck and prosperity; and especially nine, which is associated with longevity and eternity. The number nine, pronounced *kao* (เก้า), is the triple of the lucky number three and *kao* can also mean "take a step forward," so the number nine also symbolizes progress toward the future.

King Rama IX, who died in 2016 after a 70-year reign, was revered by the Thai people. His birth date even became Father's Day. The number nine was closely associated with his reign, making it very lucky indeed!

OTHER SYMBOLIC DESSERTS

Desserts other than the nine detailed at right can also represent the love between the couple and be presented as offerings to the bride and groom. These include the duo of fish *khanom pla khu* (ขนมปลาคู่) and the braided bread *khanom kong* (ขนมกง).

A monk uses the number nine to bless the opening of a building.

The nine wedding desserts are called golden desserts or thong (ทอง) because gold is associated with wealth and symbolizes prosperity for the couple. The desserts are presented together on a tray to the newlyweds, so they can receive the blessings symbolized by each.

Thong yip (ทองหยิบ) is a dessert whose name literally means "everything you touch turns to gold." It is made with flour and duck egg yolks and is cooked in a jasmine-scented sugar syrup. It is shaped like a five-pointed star.

Thong yod (ทองหยอด), or golden drops, represents perpetual wealth, as the drops never stop falling. This dessert symbolizes financial stability throughout the couple's life. It tastes similar to *thong yip* but looks quite different.

Foy thong (ฝอยทอง), with its long golden strands, symbolizes eternal love and the couple's longevity. It is prepared by passing duck egg yolks through a fine sieve into a fragrant sugar syrup. The noodles are then gathered up with a stick and formed into nests.

Thong ek (ทองเอก) symbolizes the fidelity between the bride and groom. It is a mixture of flour, coconut milk, duck egg yolks and sugar.

Med kanoun (เม็ดขนุน) represents the couple's support for each other. It is a sweet puree made of mung beans and coconut that is soaked in duck egg yolk and then in jasmine sugar syrup.

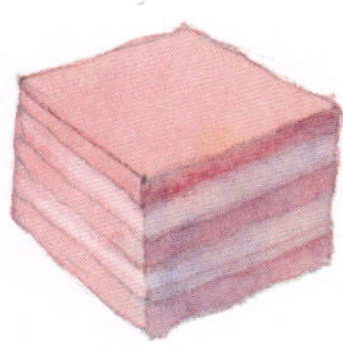

Kanom chan (ขนมชั้น) is a nine-tiered jelly cake traditionally flavored with coconut milk and pandan. It represents the couple's ability to create a home and is sometimes dyed with pink food coloring.

Dara thong (ดาราทอง) is a dessert created in the royal kitchens. Its name means "golden star." Its crown-like shape symbolizes a successful career. Making this dessert on a *thong ek* base is a long and complex process. It is characterized by its little crown made of sugar-coated watermelon seeds.

Sanay chan (เสน่ห์จันทน์) represents the newlyweds' love life being as bright as the moon illuminating the night. It is flavored with nutmeg.

Kanom thuay fu (ขนมถ้วยฟู) represents the couple's growing love and prosperity. *Fu* (ฟู) means "elevation." This small jasmine-scented steamed rice cake is colored and flavored with plant extracts such as butterfly pea flower, pandan leaf and hibiscus.

THE THAI NEW YEAR
สงกรานต์

The Thai New Year, called *songkran* (สงกรานต์), is a celebration based on the lunar calendar and begins on April 13th and lasts three days. It is the most important time of the year for Thais, and they usually take a week's vacation to celebrate with their families. It is a Buddhist celebration that is also observed in neighboring countries that share the Theravada tradition, such as Burma, Cambodia and Laos.

Songkran was originally a religious festival that involved purifying with water to welcome the new year and let go of the previous one. After cleaning their homes and other living spaces, people go to the temple (*wat*; วัด) to listen to the monks' prayers, make offerings to "earn" karmic credit and pour holy water over the statue of Buddha. The following day, people pour water on the hands of their elders to honor them and to receive their blessings for the coming year.

The new year is also a time for family reunions: People do not hesitate to cross the country to see their parents.

Families feast on their favorite dishes, which are usually prepared in large quantities and shared with neighbors and visitors. The *khao che* (ข้าวแช่), which consists of a bowl of rice soaked in iced water scented with jasmine flower, is very popular during new year's celebrations.

After observing the religious rituals and honoring one's family, it is time to celebrate and have fun! April is the hottest time of the year in Thailand, and the pouring of holy water turns into a gigantic three-day water fight in the streets. Entire buckets of water are thrown at passers-by and cars — no one is safe!

LOY KRATHONG: THE FESTIVAL OF LIGHTS (ลอยกระทง)

Loy Krathong (ลอยกระทง) is one of the country's most important celebrations. It takes place on the evening of the full moon of the 12th lunar month, in November, and marks the end of the rainy season. The celebration can extend over three days and includes parades. It began in the north of the country, and many stories surround its origins. Today, it is celebrated to thank the water goddess Phra Mae Khongkha and to commemorate Buddha.

Loy Krathong is celebrated with floating boats made from elaborately weaved banana leaves and flowers that are adorned with a candle and incense in honor of Buddha. A coin can be placed on the boat to ensure good luck in the future, together with a lock of hair or a piece of fingernail to show that the past is being released. Releasing a *krathong* onto the water symbolizes the letting go of past resentments.

Loy (ลอย) means "to float," and *krathong* (กระทง) means a small boat or basket. *Krathong* are generally shaped like lotus flowers, but the most impressive are shaped like a stupa (a dome-shaped Buddhist shrine).

According to popular folklore, this tradition dates back to the 14th century and the Sukhothai Kingdom. Nang Noppamas, a concubine of King Phra Ruang, is said to have been the first to make a beautifully decorated lotus-shaped *loy krathong* to celebrate Buddha. Since then, beauty contests in her honor have been organized during the festivities. However, evidence also suggests this ceremony existed among the neighboring Khmers in the 12th century. While others link it to Diwali, the Indian festival of lights, which celebrates the goddess associated with the Ganges. The festival's exact origins are a true mystery!

Loy Krathong is also a festival celebrated by lovers: It is said that couples will be able to meet again in their next life if they release a *krathong* together ...

khao chè

REGIONAL FESTIVALS

PHUKET'S VEGETARIAN FESTIVAL

This celebration of vegetarianism traces its origins to the Chinese community on Phuket Island. It begins on the ninth day of the ninth month of the lunar calendar. It is both a Taoist and a Buddhist celebration, paying homage to the stellar deities of the nine emperor kings and following the eight principles of the Mahayana Buddhism currently practiced in China — including not taking any human or animal life.

A PHUKET PHENOMENON

In 1825, an opera troupe from China performing in Phuket fell seriously ill. To recover, the artists turned to their religion, praying to the nine emperor kings and adopting a strict diet usually reserved for monks. When they recovered, the community was moved to establish an annual celebration in honor of their miraculous return to health.

According to local lore, on the ninth day of the ninth month of the lunar calendar, the nine emperor kings descend to visit their earthly temples. At this time, they may choose to take over the bodies of humans, conferring extraordinary powers on them. In Phuket, this belief gives rise to some impressive piercing demonstrations!

The festival has spread throughout Thailand, particularly the larger cities, where many residents have Chinese ancestry. The festival has grown to such an extent that nearly 10 million people across the country now take part in it. For nine days, people purify themselves by adopting the *je* diet (เจ), which is even more strict than a vegan diet, as it also excludes things like onions, garlic and alcohol (see p. 16). Street vendors swap their usual fare for *je* menus, indicating their participation in the event with small red-and-yellow flags.

THE CHIANG MAI LANTERN FESTIVAL

The lantern festival is celebrated in the region once covered by the ancient Lanna Kingdom, and it is arguably the country's most charming celebration. It takes place at the same time as the Loy Krathong festival, and the fact that both festivals are also held in the north often leads to confusion.

Khom kwen (โคมแขวน)

The lantern festival, called Yi Peng (ยี่เป็ง) in reference to the date it is celebrated during the Lanna calendar, has its own particular traditions. It was originally also a festival in honor of Buddha. The floating lanterns, called *khom loy* (โคมลอย), mark the end of the rainy season and the beginning of the dry season. They also symbolize the passage from darkness to light. It is believed that when the lanterns float up toward the sky, they take all the difficulties of the past with them. For three days, everyone busies themselves getting ready, hanging multicolored paper lanterns (*khom kwen*; โคมแขวน) outside their homes and the temples. Families also go to the temple to make offerings and gain merit for the next life.

On the last evening, at nightfall, the long-awaited moment arrives: the unique and enchanting spectacle of the lanterns being released. The streets are also lined with thousands of candles along the ground, symbolizing wisdom and guiding existence toward the light.

DESSERTS AND BEVERAGES

Thais do not finish a meal with dessert, but they may refresh their palate with some fresh fruit or fruit in syrup. They are, however, enthusiastic foodies and enjoy nibbling on sweets throughout the day. They also have a tradition of elaborate pastries that are specially made for celebrations and ceremonies. Many of these blend techniques learned from Portuguese immigrants with local products. Pandan leaf combined with coconut milk is the flavor of choice in many desserts. Vegetable- and fruit-based drinks are also consumed daily to quench thirst — and to enjoy as a little treat.

FRUITS (ผลไม้)

With the profusion and variety of fruits available in Thailand, it is no surprise that they can be found at nearly every stage of a meal. Fruits are eaten in both savory and sweet dishes: banana fritters, grilled banana, green papaya salad, jackfruit or palm-fruit curry, mango and coconut sticky rice pudding ...

STICKY RICE WITH COCONUT AND MANGO

Khao niew mamuang (ข้าวเหนียวมะม่วง) is the most popular dessert in Thailand and is also enjoyed beyond its borders. There are almost 200 varieties of mango in the country, so the fruit is available year-round. However, it is during the warmest months, from March to May, that *nam dok mai*, the tastiest variety of mango, is available. This also coincides with the first harvest of sticky rice. Some shops that specialize in *khao niew mamuang* are only open at this time of year! The magic of this simple yet delicious dessert lies in the freshness of its ingredients.

Yield: 4 servings
Prep time: 20 minutes
Cook time: 35 minutes
Soak time: 4 hours or overnight

- 1¼ cups (300 ml) sticky rice
- ½ cup (125 ml) granulated sugar
- ¾ cups (200 ml) coconut cream or ¾ cups (200 ml) coconut milk + 1 tbsp. (15 ml) coconut oil
- 1 pinch salt
- 2 to 3 tbsp. (30–45 ml) shelled mature soybeans (soak overnight if using dry beans)
- 2 ripe mangoes, peeled, deseeded and diced

COCONUT SAUCE

- ½ cup (125 ml) coconut milk
- 1 tbsp. (15 ml) rice flour or cornstarch

1 Soak the sticky rice in cold water for at least 4 hours.

2 Rinse the rice several times to remove as much starch as possible. This will give you nice translucent grains after the rice is cooked.

3 To ensure even cooking, place the rice in a dish towel inside a steamer basket. Steam for 25 minutes.

4 In a saucepan over low heat, stir to combine the sugar, coconut cream and salt.

5 Once the rice is cooked, transfer it to a bowl and immediately pour the hot coconut mixture over top. Stir gently with a spatula to loosen the grains of rice and allow them to soak up the coconut mixture. Cover and let rest for 20 minutes.

6 Meanwhile, prepare the coconut sauce: Stir to combine the ingredients in a saucepan over low heat, and then turn up the heat just enough to bring the mixture to a simmer, stirring to ensure it does not catch on the bottom of the pan. When the sauce has thickened, remove it from the heat and leave it to cool.

7 Soak the soybeans in boiling water for 10 minutes and then drain them. Toast them in a dry or lightly oiled pan over medium heat until golden-brown.

8 Gently stir the rice again.

9 Divide the rice among four bowls and top with chopped mango, a drizzle of the coconut sauce and a sprinkle of crispy soybeans.

PANDAN LEAVES

The pandan leaf (*bai teuil*; ใบเตย) is to Thai desserts what vanilla is to Western ones. This aromatic plant has a delicate fragrance reminiscent of rice. It appears in a wide range of preparations, sometimes savory but usually sweet. It can flavor noodles, cakes, rice and rice-flour dishes. It also gives foods a beautiful green hue.

PANDAN SPECIALTIES

Pandan cream
Sangkaya bai teuil
สังขยาใบเตย

Pandan cookies
Khanom krok bai teuil
ขนมครกใบเตย

Pandan juice
Nam bai teuil
น้ำใบเตย

Pandan and coconut jelly
Woon kati bai teuil
วุ้นกะทิใบเตย

Pandan and coconut cream
Khanom piek poun bai teuil kati sod
ขนมเปียกปูนใบเตยกะทิสด

Pandan leaves are also woven to decorate homes and tables: They impart their fragrance, acting as natural room fresheners.

PANDAN LEAF EXTRACT (*NAM BAI TEUIL*; น้ำใบเตย)

1 Slice 5 to 10 pandan leaves.
2 Add the leaves to a blender with a bit of water. The less water you use, the more concentrated the extract will be. Blend until the leaves are thoroughly incorporated into the water.
3 Filter the mixture using cheesecloth or a fine sieve to retrieve the pandan extract.

TRADITIONAL METHOD

Finely slice the pandan leaves, place in a granite mortar and crush with the pestle. Add a little water and stir to combine before filtering to collect the extract.

DESSERTS IN SYRUP

Desserts in syrup are delicious and refreshing. They can combine fresh and candied fruit, tapioca pearls, sago pearls, soybeans, taro, colored jelly and sweet sticky rice. The ingredients are arranged in a bowl and topped with sugar syrup, sometimes with the addition of coconut milk and crushed ice. Thais mostly eat them after dark, when it is a little cooler — the perfect time to take a stroll to help you digest the evening meal!

Certain ingredients are combined to make specific desserts. However, when it comes to *ruam mit* (รวมมิตร), any combination is possible: Its name means "a gathering of friends."

This type of dessert and the stalls that serve it are called *nam keng sai* (น้ำแข็งไส), which refers to the ample crushed ice that is served with the dish. There are also crushed ice desserts simply covered in colored syrup, like shaved ice or snow cones.

Ruam mi
รวมมิตร

Water chestnuts in tapioca and syrup
Tab tim krob
ทับทิมกรอบ

Sago pearls and black soybeans
Sakou tua dam
สาคูถั่วดำ

LOD CHONG (ลอดช่อง)

Rice vermicelli with pandan extract (*lod chong*) is a dessert found throughout Southeast Asia, from Vietnam to Malaysia to Laos. The noodles are served in sugar syrup and coconut milk and topped with crushed ice. *Lod chong* means "pass through the holes" and refers to the wide-holed strainer needed to make it.

Yield: 10 servings
Prep time: 20 minutes
Rest time: 24 hours
Cook time: 1 hour

- 2 ounces (50 g) pickling lime (ensure it is food-grade calcium hydroxide, often available at Asian grocery stores)
- 8 pandan leaves
- 1½ cups (375 ml) rice flour
- 2 tbsp. (30 ml) tapioca flour
- 10 ounces (300 g) palm sugar (or about 1 cup/250 ml)
- 1⅔ cups (400 ml) coconut cream
- 1 tsp. (5 ml) cornstarch
- 1 pinch salt
- Ice cubes and water
- Crushed ice

1 The day before, mix the pickling lime with 8 cups (2 L) water. Let stand 24 hours. The next day, skim off 6 cups (1.5 L) of the limewater, ensuring you do not pick up any of the deposits from the bottom.

2 Slice the pandan leaves, and then blend them with the limewater in a blender. Strain the blended mixture, saving the liquid. Squeeze out the leaves with your hands to ensure you do not leave any pandan extract behind.

3 In a large, heavy-bottomed saucepan, stir to combine the flours and pandan extract over high heat, continuing to stir until the mixture thickens. Lower the heat to medium and continue to stir until you obtain a uniform paste.

4 Cover and cook over a low heat for 45 minutes, stirring 3 times every 15 minutes. The paste should have the consistency of a thick sauce.

5 Place a *lod chong* strainer or any large-holed strainer over a large bowl filled with ice water. Pass the paste through the strainer, pressing if necessary. Pandan vermicelli will form when it hits the ice water. Strain the water to collect the pandan vermicelli.

6 Prepare the palm sugar syrup: Melt the sugar in 1¼ cups (300 ml) water. Let cool.

7 Prepare the coconut sauce: Heat the coconut cream with the cornstarch and salt until simmering. Let cool off the heat.

8 Divide the pandan vermicelli among 10 bowls, and add about 2 tbsp. (30 ml) syrup and 3 tbsp. (45 ml) coconut sauce to each serving. Top with crushed ice. Enjoy chilled!

ROYAL DESSERTS

The royal kitchens have had a major influence on Thai desserts, notably through the popularization of foreign techniques. Products imported by Portuguese immigrants have become widespread, such as cassava, which is used to produce tapioca. European techniques have also been adopted, such as the use of eggs in desserts, which marked a turning point in Thailand's gastronomic history.

WHO IS MARIA GUYOMAR DE PINA, THE QUEEN OF DESSERTS?

Maria Guyomar de Pina, called Thao Thong Kip Ma (ท้าวทองกีบม้า) in Thai, was born in 1682, in the Ayutthaya Kingdom. The daughter of an exiled Japanese Catholic mother and a father of Portuguese, Bengali and Japanese descent, she married a Greek adventurer who was elevated to the nobility by King Narai. She was well established and worked as a chef in the royal kitchens. She introduced many desserts from the Portuguese community to royal tables and is notable for having used refined sugar and duck eggs. These pastries have since become classics of Thai cuisine.

Foy thong (ฝอยทอง) is the Thai version of the Portuguese *fios de ovos* (literally "golden angel hair"). *Thong yip* (ทองหยิบ), meanwhile, is derived from the recipe for *trouxas das caldas*, although it is shaped differently.

Royal desserts are often smoked with a *tian op* candle (เทียนอบ), which gives them a smoky aroma of floral incense.

Khanom mo keng (ขนมหม้อแกง) is a coconut flan inspired by *tigelada*, the Portuguese flan.

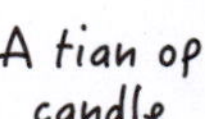

FRUIT CARVING

Fruit carving (*kan ke salak pola mai*; การแกะสลักผลไม้) is elevated to an art form in Thailand! This ancient tradition is a legacy of the royal kitchens of the Sukhothai Kingdom (13th to 15th centuries). Carved fruits and vegetables decorated royal tables, where food had to satisfy the mouth, the eyes and the heart. This discipline is still taught in cooking schools today and is considered a treasure of Thailand's gastronomic culture. Artists can express both their creativity and their cultural identity, paying homage to their birthplace.

Fruits and vegetables are carved with floral motifs of great complexity and elegance, so all can see just how sophisticated the royal court truly is.

FROZEN DESSERTS

Thailand's climate is hot all year round, and locals do just about everything they can to keep cool. One of Bangkok's favorite activities is to stroll through the many shopping malls to take advantage of the air-conditioning. In a country where the heat can be blazing, frozen desserts are a must!

COCONUT ICE CREAM (*ITIM KATI SOD*; ไอติมกะทิสด)

Traditional ice-cream vendors offer just one flavor: handcrafted coconut. They usually travel through the streets with their cart, signaling their presence with a familiar little bell that everyone recognizes!

Foreigners are often surprised when they first try Thai ice cream, since it is not served in a cone but rather between bread—like a sandwich! These sandwiches are complemented with toppings such as corn, roasted peanuts, adzuki beans, palm fruit in syrup, herb jelly or sticky rice and then drizzled with sweetened condensed milk.

It is also popular to serve coconut ice cream in a coconut shell.

Coconut ice-cream sandwich
itim khanom pang
ไอติมขนมปัง

Did You Know?

The history of ice cream in Thailand dates back over 150 years, when an official with trading posts in Singapore introduced it to King Rama IV. For a long time, only the very rich could afford imported ice cream. The first Thai frozen desserts were simply crushed ice drizzled with palm sugar syrup. Thailand's first ice-cream factory opened in 1905. Today, Thailand is the leading exporter of ice cream in Asia, and the ice-cream market is growing both inside and outside the country. Thais' ability to create innovative ice-cream products continues to generate curiosity, such as stir-fried ice cream, which is now being exported all over the world.

FROZEN SYRUP (*ITIM LOD*; ไอติมหลอด)

Another popular traditional frozen dessert is water syrup or soda pop frozen in a tube. These treats cost about 5 baht (about 15 cents) each and are very refreshing. To make them, cylinder-shaped metal molds are submerged in a barrel filled with ice water. The barrel is rotated one way and then the other, producing a characteristic sound. After a few minutes, the sweet liquid freezes, creating ice pops.

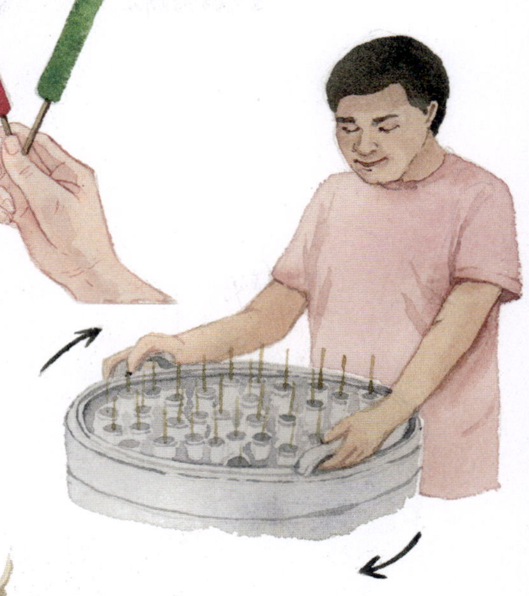

3-D ICE CREAM

Thailand's latest frozen sensation is 3-D ice-cream pops from Pop Icon, which celebrate the country's culture. The first pop, launched in 2023, reproduced the mosaic flowers of the Wat Arun temple. It was a huge success, and these icy treats have since depicted Bangkok's Chinatown, the historic site of Ayutthaya and even the *wai*, the Thais' hands-pressed-together greeting. The flavors are also traditionally Thai: tamarind, tea, mango-passion fruit and the like.

STIR-FRIED ICE CREAM (*ITIM PAD*; ไอติมผัด)

The Thais' sense of fun and spectacle is matched only by their creativity! In terms of ice cream, another new star on the market is stir-fried ice cream, also called rolled ice cream. Sweetened condensed milk and fruit are spread out on an ice-cold metal sheet. The mixture is alternately chopped and spread until it freezes. A spatula is then used to loosen the ice cream, forming a roll, like a jelly roll. Sauces and other toppings provide the finishing touch.

ALCOHOLIC BEVERAGES

Thailand has a vibrant nightlife, and Thais have a great sense of fun. They enjoy a good drink, often getting together after work and staying out late into the night. They are fans of lager and often pair beer with spicy snacks, and they also appreciate spirits and cocktails.

BEERS

The beer market is mainly divided between three brands of Thai lager: Singha, Leo and Chang. Each label features an iconic animal: a mythical lion, a leopard and two elephants, respectively.

Singha (*Sing*; สิงห์) is the oldest beer brewed in Thailand, dating back to 1933. It is a bit more expensive than the others, and it is also considered to be the best quality beer. Leo beer is from the same brewery as Singha, but it is less expensive and has more than half the market share. Chang beer is also very popular with Thais.

Did You Know?

In Thailand, beers are often served over ice—lots of ice! The ice cubes fill the glass and keep the beer cool in the sweltering heat. Beers contain 5% alcohol and are considered refreshing drinks to accompany meals. As soon as your glass is half empty, a waiter will surly fill it with more ice cubes and beer.

SPIRITS

Although all types of spirits can be found in Thailand, domestic whiskies and rums, which are less expensive than imported products, are the most popular. They have a distinctive flavor and unique characteristics. Whiskies are made from sugar and rice molasses, while rums are distilled from sugarcane. They contain on average 35% abv.

Mekhong and Hong Thong are the brands that dominate the whisky market. SangSom is the leading brand of Thai rum.

Whiskies and rums can be drunk on the rocks but are best enjoyed with soda over ice.

RICE ALCOHOL (*LAO KHAO*; เหล้าขาว)

In the countryside, locals produce their own alcohol by fermenting white rice or sticky rice. This drink is called *lao khao*, which means "white alcohol," referring to the color of the rice. It has an abv between 30% and 50% and is sometimes infused with herbs to make a traditional medicine. In that form it is called *ya dong* (ยาดอง), which means "medicinal infusion."

RED BULL: A THAI BRAND

Red Bull, the world's third best-selling non-alcoholic beverage after Coca Cola and Pepsi, originated in Thailand. It was developed in the 1970s by Chaleo Yoovidhya, a pharmaceutical representative. He wanted to create a beverage that could help energize workers.

In Thai it is called *Krating Daeng* (กระทิงแดง), or two buffaloes, as seen on the logo. In the 1980s, Austrian Dietrich Mateschitz discovered the drink on a trip to Thailand. He partnered with the Thai creator to rework the recipe and adapt it for the Western palate, notably by carbonating it. It is an energy drink, and the main ingredients are caffeine, taurine, vitamins and sugar.

Red Bull was launched in Europe in 1987 and, unlike the Thai version, was initially aimed at a wealthy customer base at luxury ski resorts. It quickly became an international success. Today, the brand has made its co-creators multi-billionaires and is still 51% owned by the Thai family and 49% by the Austrian family.

FRUIT AND VEGETABLE JUICES

FRUIT JUICES

Mixed fresh fruit juices (*nam polamai pan*; น้ำผลไม้ปั่น) are very popular beverages found all over Thailand. Fruit is sometimes mixed with vegetables, such as carrots, celery or spinach. The most popular fruits for juices are mango, watermelon, pineapple, dragon fruit, melon and coconut.

Freshly squeezed fruit juices (*nam polamai*; น้ำผลไม้) are also very popular. Pomegranate and orange are among the favorites, and they are sold in small bottles on street corners.

HERBAL TEAS AND INFUSIONS

Thailand offers many hot or iced infusions made from fruit, dried flowers or aromatic plants that help keep folks hydrated and promote good health. Among the most popular are infusions of tamarind, bael fruit, butterfly pea flower, chrysanthemum, hibiscus, lemongrass and cane sugar.

Bael juice
Nam matoom
น้ำมะตูม

Longan juice
Nam lum yai
น้ำลำไย

Pandan juice
Nam bai teuil
น้ำใบเตย

Hibiscus tea
Nam krathieb
น้ำกระเจี๊ยบ

Butterfly pea flower tea
Nam dok anchan
น้ำดอกอัญชัน

TEAS AND COFFEES

Teas (*cha*; ชา) and coffees (*cafe*; กาแฟ) are consumed both hot and iced in numerous variations.

"sock-type" coffee filter
Tungtom
ถุงต้ม

There are *boran* (ancient) varieties of tea and coffee. *Boran* tea is made with Chatramue brand tea powder, which has a unique flavor. *Boran* coffee is made with *oliang*-type coffee powder. The powder is mixed with hot water and then filtered through a sock-shaped filter. Sweetened condensed milk and evaporated milk are added, and the drink is served hot or over ice. In recent years, coffeeshops with trendy decor have sprung up in cities all over the country, offering local and imported coffee beans and a variety of lattes, Americanos and exceptional cappuccinos.

ICED COFFEE (*CAFE YEN*; กาแฟเย็น)

Yield: 1 serving
Prep time: 2 minutes

- 2 servings ground espresso beans
- 2 to 4 tbsp. (30–60 ml) sweetened condensed milk
- 1 tbsp. (15 ml) unsweetened evaporated milk
- Ice cubes

1 Prepare 1 double espresso in a coffee machine.

2 Pour the sweetened condensed milk into a tall glass and fill with ice cubes.

3 Add the hot coffee and finish with the evaporated milk. Serve immediately.

Caroline Trieu is from Southeast Asia, and Thailand has been her adopted home for more than 15 years. She learned to cook from the women in her family and is passionate about passing on traditional techniques and the right balance of flavors at her cooking workshops in Rennes, France. She shares her recipes and cooking secrets through the *Taste of Mekong* blog.

Kanchanok Inprung, also known as "Mew," is a Thai illustrator. After a career in interior design in Bangkok, she settled in Phetchaburi, where she has had her studio for more than 10 years. Phetchaburi is a city steeped in history and a gastronomic capital that was recognized by UNESCO in 2021. Mew has developed a range of projects promoting her country's cultural and gastronomic heritage.

I would like to thank Mew from the bottom of my heart for her professionalism, talent and dedication to this magnificent project! Her authentic drawings capture the life and gastronomic landscape of Thailand with great realism and emotion. A sincere friendship was born from this collaboration. I now wish readers much enjoyment on this culinary journey to the Land of Smiles. May your reading revive sweet memories or invite you to discover the most beautiful country that is so dear to my heart.

Caroline มะลิ Trieu

ขอขอบคุณ คุณออเรรี บรรณาธิการ ของ แมงโก เอดิชั่นส์ ที่ไว้วางใจในผลงานของดิฉัน ขอบคุณ คุณแคโรไลน์ ผู้เขียน ที่คอยช่วยเหลือ สื่อสารและเป็นที่ปรึกษาที่ดีตลอดใน กระบวนการทำงาน รวมถึงกำลังใจจากทุกคนในครอบครัวของเธอด้วย ขอบคุณทุกๆคนในทีม งานที่ทำให้โครงการสำเร็จไปได้ด้วยดี ขอบคุณครอบครัว ญาติพี่น้อง เพื่อนๆของดิฉันที่คอย สนับสนุน และหวังว่าทุกคนที่ได้อ่านหนังสือเล่มนี้ จะมีความสุขกับอาหารไทย และได้รับ ประทานอาหารไทยอย่างเอร็ดอร่อยค่ะ

"Thanks to Aurélie, publisher at Editions Mango, for her confidence in my work. Thanks to Caroline, the author, for her help with communication and her good advice throughout the process. Thanks also to all the members of her family for their encouragement. Thanks to every member of the team who made this project a success. Thanks to my family and friends for their support. I hope that everyone who reads this book will enjoy Thai food as much as I enjoyed eating delicious dishes throughout the project."

Kanchanok Inprung

A FIREFLY BOOK

Published by Firefly Books Ltd. 2025
First published in French by Mango, Paris, France — 2024

Translated by Nancy Foran

First printing

Published in Canada by
Firefly Books Ltd.
50 Staples Avenue, Unit 1
Richmond Hill, Ontario
L4B 0A7

Published in the United States by
Firefly Books (U.S.) Ltd.
P.O. Box 1338, Ellicott Station
Buffalo, New York
14205

Printed in China | E

We gratefully acknowledge the financial support of the Government of Canada for our publishing program.

Library of Congress Control Number: 2025932487

Library and Archives Canada Cataloguing in Publication
Title: Thai cuisine : recipes and anecdotes from Thai gastronomic culture / written by Caroline Trieu ; illustrated by Kanchanok Inprung.
Other titles: Cuisine thaïe illustrée. English
Names: Trieu, Caroline, author. | Inprung, Kanchanok, illustrator.
Description: Translation of: La cuisine thaïe illustrée. | Text in English. Includes some text in Thai.
Identifiers: Canadiana 20250159244 | ISBN 9780228105848 (softcover)
Subjects: LCSH: Cooking, Thai. | LCSH: Cooking, Thai—Pictorial works. | LCGFT: Cookbooks.
Classification: LCC TX724.5.T5 T7513 2025 | DDC 641.59593—dc23